FORECASTING
W I T H
OUT-LIARS

MITIGATING BLAME, BIAS, AND APATHY IN YOUR
PLANNING PROCESS TO DRIVE MEANINGFUL AND
SUSTAINABLE FINANCIAL IMPROVEMENTS

J O H N   M I N K

Published by Mindstir Media, LLC
45 Lafayette Rd | Suite 181| North Hampton, NH 03862 | USA
1.800.767.0531 | www.mindstirmedia.com

ISBN-13: 978-1-7368410-1-3

Printed in the United States of America

*Dedicated to my Supply Chain and
Operations colleagues all over the world
whose tireless efforts and
personal sacrifice rarely get
the recognition they deserve.
You have my deepest respect and admiration.*

Acknowledgements

To **my family** — my wonderful wife Debbie and our two daughters Megan and Kelly. You have witnessed my trials and tribulations throughout my career, and without your support and love, I would be nothing. I love you all.

To **Barbara McNichol** — thank you for taking my incoherent scribble and turning this into an intelligible read.

To **Pat Murray** — the best Supply Chain tag team partner I ever had the pleasure to work with. Looking forward to the next lobster dinner.

To **Russ Henning** — Not only are you a great Horn Instructor, being able to leverage your other talents have been invaluable to me. Thank you for a second set of eyes.

To **Jen McNabney** and the **Mindstir Media team** — thank you for your partnership by turning my thoughts into something tangible.

Table of Contents

Foreword

I played "Beat the Mink" and lost! In Chapter 4 the author, John Mink, describes a contest he ran with his co-workers called "Beat the Mink". In the chapter, John competed against his co-workers in a forecasting contest with the prize being a free beer. When I played "Beat the Mink" the stakes where much higher as it cost me 3lb lobster at one of the finest restaurants in downtown Chicago. I was more than happy to pay my debt for John literally saved the company millions of dollars.

In Forecasting with Out-Liars, John details his learnings over twenty years of Sales and Operations Planning (S&OP) experience. John and I worked together over a ten-year period at two different companies. During that time, John lived the lessons he evangelizes in this book and I witnessed the dramatic financial and customer experience improvements he helped champion with his methods. In Forecasting with Out-liars, John provides a practical approach to the S&OP process starting with culture and collaboration vs. data and functional responsibility.

This book is a great example of a hands-on approach to the S&OP process that focuses on the human elements of the process. Forecasting with Out-liars is not only ideal for Supply Chain professionals, but for any experienced business leader as well.

Patrick Murray
Vice President of Global Supply Chain at Resideo

Introduction

"... because of supply chain issues!"

This phrase, used countless times in our businesses, triggers great anxiety for me. It automatically focuses attention on a symptom and implies blame on a specific group. Countless wasteful hours are spent on CYAs ("covering your asses"), finding fault elsewhere, attempting to hold some person or group accountable, creating discord that build walls in the organization, thus negatively affecting a company's culture.

Yes, every company has and will have supply chain issues, but many times the root cause lies *inside* the Sales and Operations Planning (S&OP) process—specifically when developing the demand forecast. Companies invest significant time and dollars developing and improving the S&OP process, but outcomes often fail to meet expectations.

It continues to astonish me how many businesses treat and manage demand forecasting. If the business is well connected, the demand forecast is the key driver to make decisions on capacity, purchases, and inventory plans. Yet, I have seen this process become apathetic, more of a "check-the-box" exercise when significant and sustainable cost and customer service-level improvements can be made. With proper investments and a focus on structure, culture, and—most important—talent, bottom-line and cash flow improvements will result.

I feel compelled to write this book because of the journey I have taken in the S&OP process and dealing with the execution problems it can manifest. My experience has been mainly in the manufacture, distribution, and sales of material goods, but all subjects here apply to pure service industries too. What this book provides is a different perspective to help you deal with planning process realities in a diverse, constructive manner.

Applying more than twenty years of Planning responsibility over my career, I have tested, learned, and developed methods that drove better outcomes for the businesses I have worked for. What has worked? Modifying mindsets and coping with the realities of human behavior has altered my actions and thoughts so I could assist in improving outcomes that become sustainable. This book aims to do exactly that.

No matter what the maturity level of your company's forecasting processes, you can always find room for improvement. Looking at the processes through a fresh lens can benefit your customer experience and financials immensely. Through the learning journey described in this book, I share experiences in how forecasts are influenced and how they can be improved by weeding out the biases that inherently exist. Along the way, I challenge traditional organizational thinking about what can sustain business results via improving the S&OP process. As you will uncover, you will realize how your organization's culture makes or breaks this process. But do not expect this book to wave a magic wand over your processes to make everything work. Instead, expect a journey of small, integrated steps—involving people as well as processes.

You may be wondering, "What about systems such as Enterprise Resource Planning (ERPs), cloud-based tools, and Artificial Intelligence in our company, John?" Systems are vital, but many times they are used as excuses for why a business cannot perform or make better decisions. Often, companies do not fully leverage the existing systems they have already invested in. Always searching for the next best system to solve forecasting issues can be an enabler once it is implemented, but systems cannot manage the human behaviors that drive the key decisions companies make. That is why this book focuses on *people* and *processes*, which rarely get the same attention or headlines as systems do.

On these pages, I share several experiences on my journey and how I addressed the challenges posed while offering alternative approaches to improve your planning process and business results. Read on!

Chapter 1:

What Is S&OP?

Sales and Operations Planning (S&OP). Integrated Business Planning (IBP). Sales, Inventory, and Operations Planning (SIOP)... No matter what name you call it, these are fundamentally the same processes that attempt to align a company's demand and supply needs so it can drive a business plan to (1) set and achieve profit and loss goals, (2) determine balance sheet expectations, and (3) drive operational decisions for capacity, purchasing, and inventory.

The premise of these processes is simple:

1. Develop and align on one demand signal.
2. Vet supply to the demand signal; determine what demand can and cannot be met.
3. Make key business decisions, action plans, and trade-offs.
4. Determine/revise the Operating Plan and Financial Forecast with supply constraints.
5. Review lessons learned previously to drive improvement.
6. Rinse and repeat.

The first crucial area of the S&OP process is the development and creation of the demand signal. The demand signal is then translated into the supply signal, which drives the need to purchase material, plan capacity and resources, and determine constraints where demand cannot be met. When it comes down to it, those in the Supply Chain bear the responsibility of meeting sales order shipment dates, expediting and/or reprioritizing supply, keeping proper inventory levels, and managing overall operational costs. Yet many of these stakeholders in Supply

Chain may have little or no input to the demand signal — which drives all the Supply Chain activity!

S&OP is a common-sense approach, and many companies have formally adopted the steps noted here. Consulting firms specialize in helping leaders define the process, assist in change management, and develop the operating rhythm and metrics to define success. As a result, leaders expect to see improvements around implementing the S&OP process, yet often, advances are indistinguishable compared with previous processes. Items such as revenue, profit, balance sheet, and customer satisfaction show no improvement and might even become worse. So, leaders abandon this approach or put the process on autopilot—the "checking-the-box" approach—in which they claim they have a process, but it is perceived as having no real teeth and/or business value.

Still, many companies do make the S&OP process work well. I believe the key ingredients for success are (1) a solid organizational structure with clear roles, responsibilities, and realistic measures, (2) strong talent, and (3) a culture in which hard decisions are made to avoid a detrimental outcome. This map may be difficult to follow, but I have worked in organizations where I have witnessed the S&OP process embraced, organized properly, and drive proactive decisions. Leaders avoided the pitfalls of consuming the organization in "firefighting" (being reactive), which severely hampers the entire process.

> ## To be successful, the "art" of the S&OP process needs to complement the "science."

Many times, the S&OP process is viewed as solely Supply Chain's responsibility. But, realistically, Supply Chain personnel point to a *poor demand forecast* as the key reason for not meeting expectations. Even if the members of the Supply Chain are involved or chair the demand reviews, they usually have little success in influencing the demand itself. Questions abound:

☑ How could someone in Supply Chain understand what is going on in the market?

☑ How well does someone in Supply Chain know the product and the customers' needs?

☑ Sales and Marketing are in the best position to determine demand, aren't they?

Questions like these reflect traditional thinking that drive an artificial division of roles and responsibilities that many companies simply cannot get past.

As I gained experience in managing the S&OP process, it became noticeably clear the creation of the demand signal was plagued with bias. Whether through basic lack of understanding of potential consequences (ignorance), personal agendas, individual egos, or simple apathy, these contributed to a biased demand signal. Bias makes an inherently poor demand signal even worse, yet the process can be buried several layers down in an organization. Often, it is not well understood how the demand signal even came into fruition.

So, a new set of questions emerge:

☑ How is demand bias developed?

☑ How are S&OP realities analyzed?

☑ What practical measures can be implemented to improve the demand signal?

Please do not let me mislead you. Biases will always exist. The objective is to keep biases to a minimum with the goal of improving business outcomes. Perceived as being either bold or insane, as I advanced my career, I made sure any company I joined who made me accountable for inventory, on-time shipping, and operational costs - my team and I had would also be responsible for the demand signal. *This mindset eventually paid big dividends (literally) for the entire organization.*

What did this new mindset require? Solid leadership and interpersonal skills, but just as important, extraordinarily strong cross-functional collaboration. Robust collaboration does not happen overnight, but small successes add up, build trust, and help knock down organization and people barriers. In the chapters that follow, I suggest how you can drive your company toward the ideal: *extraordinarily strong cross-functional collaboration*.

Chapter 2:
The Vicious Circle of Blame

It finally happened. The great big sales order for one of the largest new accounts just came in—and as usual, near the end of the fiscal year. Phew! This big order was part of our financial forecast and was needed to achieve our quarterly revenue target along with the super-thin margins that came with winning such a high-profile account. Although those in Supply Chain were rushed to deliver; they planned for it—and promised to ship by the end of the quarter. Start popping the champagne!

But even as emails circulated with congratulations from the CEO, something was amiss. The sales order had different stock keeping units (SKUs) than planned, and the order showed accessories that were not forecasted. So, to meet the shipment deadline for the end of the quarter, Supply Chain manufactured a completely different SKU and did not have the accessories available to meet the order.

Furthermore, the customer wanted the units shipped individually to each of its physical retail locations. Many were located across country borders where we had not shipped before in any large scale. On top of this were different incoterms (a set of internationally recognized rules defining who is responsible for paying for and managing the shipment, insurance, documentation, customs clearance, and other logistical activities on the order). They called for FOB Delivery, meaning revenue could not be booked until the customer received the product. In this case, the Supply Chain planned to be able to ship until the last day of the quarter and still recognize the revenue.

As the sales orders were loaded in the system, the commitment dates came back stating the orders would ship 13 weeks from that time! The account manager quickly called up the customer service representative who verified that fact. The emails escalated, and the celebration quickly turned into a mob lynching. The stereotypical demands began: "We need to hold someone accountable!" So did the blame: "Again, the Supply Chain dropped the ball" and "This order was forecasted, and Supply Chain committed to ship but can't!"

The head of Supply Chain, having to answer for this fiasco, sent the organization into a flurry of activity to find out what happened. The goal for this person was to ensure the Supply Chain team was aligned and executing to what it had been agreed to. He/she had to follow all the proper internal protocols while she/he fielded phone calls and emails on why the Supply Chain organization was "worthless". The shouting matches at the executive level started, thus the beginning of a vicious circle of blame.

As the frustration mounted, information trickled in. The SKU that was forecast was changed with the aid of the Product Manager who pointed out the new SKU had a lower cost and still had the features the customer needed. The salesperson was able to influence the customer to purchase this new SKU. The Product Manager had cc'd two Supply Chain team members on an email three weeks before, but the message did not flow to the correct Supply Chain team member(s). The new SKU had not been changed in the demand planning system. Also, the accessories on the order were not forecasted or planned for.

It was also uncovered that one email was sent to a Customer Service Representative (not part of Supply Chain) from the salesperson stating the sales order will be broken out into each of the customer's store locations and product needed to be shipped directly to each of them. This email did not mention the incoterms, and the Customer Service Representative did nothing with the email. However, that person had been on vacation when the email had been sent and was still "catching up".

Not surprisingly, when the quarterly earnings were announced, the expected revenue was not achieved "...due to supply chain issues."

Can you relate to stories like this—ones that bring up a lot of emotion and frustration? When you look at the personnel involved individually, each person believed he/she was performing the correct measures. But at the end of the day, the sales order simply could not be executed as planned. Yet the blame game was in full swing:

▸ The Account Manager blames the Supply Chain.

▸ The Supply Chain head blames the Account Manager for the wrong SKU and no knowledge of the shipping destinations.

▸ There was no change in the demand planning system when the new SKU was introduced.

▸ Emails had been sent to all the senior leaders of the functional organizations stating Supply Chain was building the forecasted SKU to hit financial quarter's revenue, setting a firm expectation.

▸ The Account Manager said the SKU was changed weeks before and pointed to the Product Manager who pointed to the email about the SKU change that went to "Supply Chain". The Product Manager assumed the two people he sent the email to would pass it on to the appropriate Supply Chain members.

▸ The Finance Manager weighed in and said they had a meeting (no Supply Chain personnel present) and agreed to change the SKU based on a better product cost structure. Now, the SKU that was produced needed to be re-worked. The thin margins that existed were completely wiped out. A loss was inevitable.

▸ On the accessory front, the Account Manager said the customer decided at the last minute the accessories they wanted to purchase. The Account Manager was not aware the customer would purchase any accessories.

▸ The Account Manager sent out a nasty email to the Supply Chain team, copying the CEO. It expressed how disappointed the customer was and accused the team of not focusing on the customer but only on internal metrics such as inventory.

Do any of these complaints sound familiar? Animosity, lack of trust, calling other functions names can spread rampantly. The company culture can suffer, and deep dives to understand what happened within the company begin. There will be a meeting with the CEO to articulate root causes and determine corrective actions, so this never happens again. Additional policies and procedures are put in place. Still, only a few months later, a similar issue repeats itself.

After several repetitions like this, Supply Chain leaders end up "pursuing new opportunities." Then the "new leader of hope" brings in the high-profile, "brand-reputable" consultants who easily point out already-known organizational and process gaps. All the while, he/she spouts out, isolated, best-in-class metrics that may be possible to achieve.

My favorite part is when consultants tell the executive team how poor the forecast accuracy is, that other firms they have consulted for perform much better—without any context about how the forecast is measured or what industry it comes from. Considerable cost and effort go into improving the forecast without tangible improvements coming out of it. Then it is time to blame the IT systems. The new idea? The company needs to invest in better systems and leverage Artificial Intelligence (AI) that will improve the demand signal. It will also take significant cost out of the business. That takes us further away from the root cause even more.

In my experience, there is no magic wand that will make the S&OP process improve. There is no simple answer. But here's food for thought. Do you have someone in your organization who has (or can grow into a position of having) enough knowledge of both the go-to market and supply chain planning processes—and can better link the two?

Many linkages need to work well to make an S&OP process effective, but this area between market knowledge and supply chain understanding is typically a chasm. This creates a large gap in understanding that focuses an organization on reactivity and blame. Sound familiar?

Yes, finding someone with this experience is easier said than done. But the company needs to invest in people who can develop a broader end-to-end end understanding—from customer fulfillment to key supplier lead times and capabilities. In my experience, this person should be in a Planning function. When companies develop their S&OP process, Supply Chain consultants will insist that the organization keep the Demand and Supply Planning teams separate. The intent is to keep demand "pure", free from biases and not constrained by any Supply Planning influence. In my experience, separating Demand and Supply Planning is an organizational mistake. Why? Because more gaps will exist between the teams and human nature will take over. In other words, a Demand Planning team will not feel the execution issues that it can create, thus giving them no further incentive to improve the signal. I have witnessed by integrating the two teams not only creates organizational efficiency, but generates a broader business understanding and develops a much better demand forecast in the end.

> *In my experience, separating demand and supply planning is an organizational mistake.*

A solid S&OP process can be leveraged ONLY if you have the right organizational competencies that invest in ways to:
- ☑ better anticipate problems and opportunities,
- ☑ grasp key issues to make solid recommendations,
- ☑ pursue a plan of action, and
- ☑ work across a multi-faceted organization.

Many companies formalize the S&OP process, yet it can lack teeth. It is difficult to find team members who can analyze issues, connect key dots, *and* make recommendations. They simply do not have both the go-to-market and supply chain experience and knowledge that is needed. Eventually, the process turns into an ineffective "check-the-box" exercise, which will perpetuate a "blame" culture.

Many professionals claim expertise in this arena but finding the knowledge and interpersonal skill set to lead it can be extremely challenging. If you find this leader, you will know immediately—and sometimes she/he may already be sitting inside your organization.

Of extreme importance is organizational clarity. In this instance, the account manager thought she/he was effectively communicating, but messages did not get to the right people at the right time. The situation in the opening story could have been avoided (partially or completely) if that right individual thought through these criteria:

- ▸ Who needs to know?
- ▸ What needs to take place?
- ▸ What are the correct questions to ask?
- ▸ What decisions that need to be made and by when?
- ▸ Realize that sending an email to "the Supply Chain" is not organizational clarity.

I share this story not because it is purely a forecasting issue (which it partially is) but to show how issues and solutions can spin a larger web of solution-seeking instead focusing on the root causes: poor communication, lack of organizational clarity, and no coordination. This is not a system's issue; it is a "people and process" issue.

> *This is not a system's issue; it is*
> *a "people and process" issue.*

In this story, no intentional sabotage went on, but the "blame game" behaviors, especially by leaders, set the tone for being able to wrestle future issues before they reach critical stages.

Poor leadership can foster a culture of "staying in your lane" which will silence the challenging of poor decisions, especially when the consequences could be damaging.

"As long as there is someone else to blame" should not be in your organization's mindset, but unfortunately, it is. No matter how good the talent and processes an organization possesses, a toxic culture will wipe out all of it.

If not actively managed, the vicious circle of blame can considerably damage your organization financially. No one wants to be called out as the person who failed; pointing blame elsewhere tends to come first. Yes, responsibility can and should be placed on an individual, but many issues are more complex and dynamic than homing in on one person.

If a significant blame culture exists in your organization, you will find it difficult for people to speak up and be proactive. There is always an "out"—someone you can point the finger toward when something fails. But blame will facilitate bias and apathy, which de-values any S&OP process and will add unnecessary costs to your company. Ask yourself, "Does my organization focus a lot of activities on pushing, deflecting, or preventing blame" versus "what efforts provide the best outcome for the business?"

What situations can you point toward in your company that contribute to a culture of blame?

Chapter 3:
Bias Runs Rampant

It was relatively early in my career. My company was the world leader in cellular phone sales, but I was watching that leadership position quickly evaporate. We finally adopted a formal S&OP process and, as a Product Manager, I got involved in the newly formed consensus demand meetings that would develop the one demand signal to drive our Supply Chain activities. As a bonus, I was given a forecast accuracy metric that I was expected to meet or exceed. (I had zero input on setting it, and it took me a while to even understand it.)

In preparation for my first consensus demand meeting, I gave my forecast on the product portfolio I was managing to the S&OP Manager. Factors I had taken into consideration were the TAM (Total Addressable Market), competitive offerings, pricing, sales history, new product introductions (and estimated delays), product quality, and customer interest. The S&OP Manager at the time used this forecast along with forecasts from the other product managers to develop the revenue and margin forecast. The resulting financial roll up of the forecast showed revenue decline and terrible margins.

This meeting brought in all the senior management personalities: VP of Operations, VP of Finance, VP of Product Management, and VP of Sales. We all knew we could not leave this meeting without creating this single demand forecast. How would we make our quarterly and yearly revenue targets and earnings with this forecast? We need to solve this!

The meeting quickly turned into a fascinating demonstration of politics while ignoring the reality that was facing us. It felt to me like an alternate reality. When I spoke about my portfolio, the analysis I shared was looked at as pessimistic—as if I were the "boy who cried wolf."

After several attempts to articulate the "facts" as I saw them, I was tuned out. I received a message from my manager via two-way pager to "just be quiet." Then our VP of Finance, in all his infinite wisdom, picked out a high-end, niche product that had excellent margins. The product was limited on the cellular networks it would work on, so the TAM was relatively small. By increasing the demand forecast on the product by five times, he said, we could achieve the revenue and margin targets set for the quarter. "There, this solves it!" exclaimed the VP of Finance.

In shock and dismay, I spoke to the facts again while my manager, who had already instructed me to "zip it," gave me the glare of death. I made these points:

- ☑ the forecast submitted for this niche product was 60% of the TAM
- ☑ a huge price cut would be needed to increase the volumes to this magnitude
- ☑ the other products in our portfolio would need be reduced in price
- ☑ the product's lifecycle had only 6 to 9 months left
- ☑ the product itself is polarizing and lacks mass consumer appeal

The VP of Finance just looked at me, pointed to the VP of Sales, and said, "Now the Sales team needs to make this happen." The VP of Sales exclaimed, "We will do our best!" Meeting adjourned.

Yes, this meeting actually happened. I questioned myself and asked, "What am I missing? With higher volumes, could the Supply Chain get a better product cost, thus we could significantly lower pricing? With Sales and Marketing rallying around this, would we get much higher sales? Would our VPs meet in a separate session and put together an execution plan? Was there a secret, high-level negotiation going on with one of our largest customers I was not aware of?"

Somehow, I did not have all the information. But we developed a "consensus" (I guess) demand forecast so the S&OP process box move forward. At the very least, I knew I would soon learn the answers to my questions.

After another "career coaching session" from my manager, we set off to execute this demand forecast. Supply Chain expedited (adding cost) the material needed and increased the manufacturing plans for the fiscal quarter. Days went by and the sales volumes inched along but nowhere near the volumes in the consensus demand forecast. Sales were even lower than my original demand forecast projection. Inventories for the product continued to build, and the company's attention turned to other avenues to fulfill the revenue and margin goals. As time went on, the inventory became my problem to fix as a new regime of VPs took over. In the meantime, several leaders moved on to "pursue new opportunities."

Even though this is an extreme example, bias does exist in every forecast because we are human beings with different agendas, knowledge, and experience. Many times, to achieve "consensus", I have witnessed the biggest personality or the highest-ranking person in the room succeeds to drive her/his position, making passionate arguments to do so. Here are a few of the many amusing quotes I have heard used to justify a position.

- "We need to drive it and let Sales finally do their job."
- "I cannot report these numbers; we will all get fired."
- "Build it, and they will come."
- "I was told by Supply Chain that if we do not forecast it, we will not have product. We need to over-forecast everything".
- "The volume we drive needs to match the business case" (developed months/years previously).
- "Someone else provide a better suggestion that meets the plan/forecast!"
- "The {insert function here} is in the best position to determine the demand plan."
- "It does not matter what we forecast; we will be wrong anyway."

▶ "We need to invest in AI (Artificial Intelligence) to create a better forecast."

Does this type of rhetoric sound familiar within your organization? Are the consequences of decisions made well understood? Are these consequences pushed to other people/ groups that took no part in the decision?

Yes, bias does exist in every forecast, but why? The answers to this question vary, but mostly they fall into three key categories:

1. Accountability
2. Lack of Knowledge
3. Politics

1. ACCOUNTABILITY

It is much easier to make decisions if the consequences do not directly affect the individual or team. Knowing we will not need to clean up the mess created by being wrong provides little motivation to drive a better outcome.

The way organizations are set up and measured can drive bias—and significantly contribute to the "blame game." A classic example of organizational thinking is: Sales is accountable for the revenue; Supply Chain is accountable for cost and inventory values. Sales will determine the demand forecast; Supply Chain will execute to it.

Yet when revenue projections are not met, Sales quickly points out that Supply Chain could not deliver. Supply Chain points out "this demand forecast was wrong" or "it wasn't forecast in the right time." When inventory is too high, Supply Chain will say the Sales forecast was flawed, that it procured parts and products incorrectly based on the forecast.

Biases may also continue to build based on issues in trying to execute shipping a sales order. For instance, if there are shortages of a product, the demand forecast bias will increase for fear of stocking out again, even if the shortage was not caused by under-forecasting the product. *Without the proper personnel, analysis, and organization able to understand*

and manage both sides of the demand and supply equation, the situation could quickly spin out of control.

2. LACK OF KNOWLEDGE

One's knowledge base also contributes to bias. Lack of key information could drive sub-optimal decisions. Variables might include lead times, sales/sell-thru history, planned promotions, sales funnels, product lifecycles, engineering changes, quality issues, returns, end of life components, product margins, field inventories, and historical demand biases. *If these variables were better understood, they could aid in developing a better forecast.*

In your organization, relevant pieces of information might be readily available, but some may be hard to find and coordinate. When execution issues occur, it is helpful to back it up and find out what information was missing when the demand decision was made. From there, obtaining that information for upcoming forecasts will only improve future outcomes.

3. POLITICS

Politics plays a key part in the forecasting process and yet is probably the hardest piece to influence. Politics can be based on someone's personal agenda, the insecurities a leader may have, or the situation a person may find himself/herself in. To provide the best *personal* outcome, human nature takes over. People tend to act, behave, and make decisions based on how they believe they will be perceived.

It would be naïve to think that politics doesn't play a major part in your S&OP process—just as naïve as believing political biases can be eliminated. The hope is that the people, process, and culture of the organization are strong enough to minimize these. All too often, this is not the case.

A skilled S&OP leader will be able recognize biases and is equipped to set up plenty of opportunities for anyone attempting to drive an erroneous decision to "save face." Putting an engaged senior leader with high emotional intelligence accountable for the S&OP process can prove to be invaluable.

That person must attempt to understand and balance customer satisfaction, revenue, cost, and working capital to neutralize problems in this arena and be able to help make the tradeoffs between these variables.

Leveraging a senior-level executive to lead your S&OP process can also address many of the biases inherent in the organization. Making healthier, proactive decisions will only help revenue, cost, and customer satisfaction. For example, having a VP/SVP of Planning may be a position that, if filled with a qualified leader, can be valuable—not only improving customer satisfaction and business results, but influencing the company culture. This leader should have a broad understanding of the customer and competitive marketplace, the products and services offered, and any supply chain constraints that pushes decision points to the forefront *before* getting into the execution window where costs can be significant. (Characteristics of a good S&OP leader are discussed in Chapter 9.)

Minimizing forecasting bias is difficult but not impossible. A good first step is recognizing it! Second, putting in measures and analysis around it looking for trends and outliers will help identify areas to investigate. Third, understanding what is driving the bias is instrumental in doing something about it.

Business professionals will always be multi-tasking and juggling responsibilities, but this is an area in which S&OP process stakeholders need to pause, think, and ask, "Is this the most accurate demand signal we can provide at this point?"

Where does bias play a role in your organization's planning process?

Chapter 4:
Beat the Mink

Well, I got what I deserved! After several "supply chain issues" on my portfolio's new product launches, I finally lost my temper. After numerous technical delays, I was at my wit's end. After finally gaining technical acceptance, we could not ship because part of the final packaging was missing a few components. Yet another delay!

After delivering one of the best rants in the history of the company, I was approached by my manager and told I would now be leading the Sales and Operations Planning (S&OP) process for our division. My Product Manager duties would be relieved from me. I believe the intent was to put me into a less stressful role and perhaps leverage my product and analytical experience in the forecasting process. Regardless, this move put me in a position to learn more about our supply chain where I could grow and learn.

Our company had invested a significant amount of time, effort, and cost into the S&OP process, but we still had many "supply chain issues." Bringing in seasoned talent to drive process improvements was next. The Region Leader decided to invest in a Customer Operations team that would focus on our key accounts. This team would establish peer to peer relationships with our top customers to manage the demand forecast and inventory availability between the two companies. This was also an attempt to remove biases inherent in previous forecasts. As a result, the Operations teams would now have input into the demand signal along with our Customers and our Sales teams.

As the new lead for S&OP, I put in forecast accuracy goals and measures, breaking them into three input categories: The Customer forecast, the Sales forecast, and the Customer Operations forecast. Having this data from each category proved to be extremely valuable, and the results were consistent in every account.

Constantly, the Customer forecast was, by far, always the worst. Taken verbatim, we would have inventory coming out of our ears. These forecasts far exceeded the actual volume that would ever sell. I believe the Customer forecasts were mainly driven by fear of running out of product.

The second worst forecast was capturing it from Sales. They could take out some of the customer bias but was still far from reaching the forecasting accuracy targets set. In this case, part of the customer bias was removed.

The third worst forecast came from the Operations team. Although statistically better than both Sales and Customer forecast, they represented a marked improvement but rarely hit the goals we set for forecast accuracy. The good news is that additional forecast bias was removed.

After a deep-dive analysis, continuous improvement plans, and some time, the Operations forecasts hit a plateau. Over time, they deteriorated somewhat. To do something "fun" and provide an incentive, I put together a program called "Beat the Mink," which lasted six months. We would add another forecast category called "the Mink forecast" and compare it to the other forecast inputs. On a monthly basis for the next for six months, the "Mink" forecast accuracy would be compared against the forecasts from the Operations team members. If an Operations forecast "Beat the Mink"—did better than the one I had set— the winning individual would get a free beer.

What were the results? The entire time, I only had to purchase two beers (and it happened to be for the same person).

As this story noted, of 48 forecast events, only twice did someone "Beat the Mink." The demand forecast I provided were statistically better than what the Operations team predicted. How could this be? Was I a genius? Was I extremely lucky? Could I predict the future? Those who know me understand I am called a genius only under certain, not-too-flattering circumstances. Those who have gambled with me know all the luck I have had was only bad. Those who know my investments would have made a lot of money by doing the exact opposite. No, I am nothing of the sort.

So how could be my forecasts be better than everyone else's when no other statistical tools or systems were involved? Furthermore, why were forecasts from the Sales team better than the Customer? And why did the Operations team have better results than Sales? The answers are both simple and complex.

I attempted to explain this phenomenon by developing a matrix. In Figure 1, I broke the analysis into four main topics

Demand Forecast Influencer	Customer	Sales	Operations	Mink
Forecast Accuracy	Worst	2nd Worst	3rd Worst	Least Worst
Agenda				
Not running out of stock	X	X	X	
Meeting New Product Introduction dates	X	X	X	
Revenue Attainment		X	X	
Pricing Concessions	X			
"Showing up" Colleagues/Not buying beer				X
Accountability				
Supplier Inventory Liability				X
Inventory Turns		X		
Customer Inventory Levels			X	X
Product Demand Forecast			X	X
Meeting Revenue Goals		X	X	
Measures (in goals)				
Forecast Accuracy			X	X
On Time Delivery			X	X
Revenue Attainment		X	X	
Trade Working Capital				X
Excess and Obsolescence				X
Other Influencers				
Market/Competitive factors		X	X	X
Sales History		X	X	X
Product Quality				X
Promotional Events/New Pricing	X	X	X	X

Figure 1

of influence: (1) agenda, (2) accountability, (3) measures, and (4) other factors could influence the forecast. From there, I characterized what the influencers were that drove the bias by group (Note that I categorized the forecast from "worst" to "least-worst," knowing forecast accuracy is typically poor and always has room for improvement.) Though demand forecasts are never perfect, supply chain strategies still need to center around how accurate and consistent these forecasts are.

As you can see under the Agenda category, the only item influencing me was my ego. I was not weighed down by other elements that may have factored in. I was also not influenced by a history of product stock outs, new product introduction dates (that never came close to hitting their mark), hitting a revenue/commission target or driving up our inventory in hopes of getting a price concession (I think some of our customers' personnel understood this well, because they would benefit from a price drop when we had too much inventory.)

Being a former Product Manager with history on new product issues, I was able to forecast the product introduction timings a lot better. Product launch dates were always aggressive and never came near to the planned launch date; however, the forecasts generated were based on the advertised date. *This was a key difference in my forecast compared to the others.* By not being tied to this, I would forecast the existing portfolio longer than planned. (If we had used my demand forecasts as the consensus forecast, it would have reduced a lot of expediting costs and/or stock outs that we eventually incurred.)

From a continuous improvement perspective, I was able to incorporate this learning and then challenge New Product Introduction (NPI) dates and portfolio effects. This did not make me popular with Engineering, Product, and Program Management (a story for a later chapter). However, the organization would have experienced better calls on the forecast as a result.

On the other hand, as far as accountability was concerned, I had factors to deal with that differed from my counterparts.

When it came to liability, I had to deal with two factors: selling the product versus scrapping parts. This was an excruciatingly painful process. Consistently, over-forecasting the demand created this excess position, which would eventually turn into price concessions and/or scrapping of material. I had to be conscious about how much we drove in our overall product forecast within material and manufacturing lead times.

Of course, all this affected the company's P&L.

Many times, if we wanted to put in an aggressive forecast, we would take down the demand forecast in future periods. That way, if the forecast did not turn out, we would have a chance to consume the liability. It would also give us time to increase the forecast if the demand forecast happened to be accurate. The S&OP purists would crucify me for this because it would screw up capacity planning. But within a certain range, capacity numbers were easier to manage than material liability. Material liability versus capacity planning issues was a conscious trade-off we made.

When it came to measures, my performance was not measured on attaining revenue but on working capital (inventory, in this case), excess and obsolescence costs, as well as on-time delivery goals. My potential bonus (with the key word being "potential") revolved around achieving these measures. Goals were based on a percentage improvement from previous years, and they ended up conflicting with one another rather than being complementary. Trying to balance these proved to be challenging, but that had to become part of my thought process and learning cycle. Having both customer satisfaction goals along with P&L and cash flow goals proved to be extremely valuable because I was not boxed into one key category such as only revenue, cost, or working capital (inventory).

Having both customer satisfaction goals along with P&L and cash flow goals proved to be extremely valuable.

I believe the S&OP team and I were the only function that had these goals. This forced us to look across these factors and examine the business like a general manager would.

Measures are extremely important *and* exceedingly difficult to align and balance within an organization.

Other factors depended on a person's experience, knowledge, competency, and personal insights—factors still influential in creating the demand forecast. I kept a pulse on competition and sales history, but I sought out product quality information, both formally and informally. (Speaking with our Customer Service Reps on customer complaints at the water cooler proved to be valuable.) The severity of product quality issues would prove to be a key indicator if a product would succeed or not.

The one key takeaway from "other factors" is that promotions and pricing activity were sometimes managed in a vacuum. Also, pricing and promotion decisions were always made inside supply chain lead times. Developing a promotional plan roadmap that would coincide with supply chain lead times may not be realistic, given the competitive nature of most industries. However, promotions should be incorporated into the demand planning process, at the very least. It leads to understanding if the supply chain can execute to promotional planned volumes. When they can align, it drives a better outcome.

Forecasting bias can be driven by many variables, and the measures set up can have unintended consequences in driving forecast bias. My thought processes on what drives bias has helped me identify the root cause behind the bias. Given this point of view, I could manage forecasts differently, which enabled us to drive a better, more beneficial outcome. It is a worthwhile exercise to do in your organization—identifying where bias comes from (including your own) and acting upon it.

How would you categorize the factors that influence *your* company's forecast bias?

Chapter 5:
Look at Us, We are Awesome!

It was dire straits at my company. We had only one real successful product, and it made up most of our sales. Unfortunately, the product was on the tail end of its lifecycle, and new technologies were emerging that we were behind on. We were heading into our last quarter of the year, which typically made up 35% to 40% of our annual revenue. We had had a decent year thus far, and we still had a chance at earning some, if not all, of our annual bonus.

Given that sales and market share were slipping away, it was decided we would drastically cut the price to position our one and only mainstream product for the holiday season. Once we implemented the new pricing, sales orders came in droves. Fantastic news! With these new orders, it looked like we would exceed the revenue target for the fiscal period, and with the high volumes, we would get better economies of scale, especially on manufacturing and consolidated freight costs.

However, one big problem lurked. The price drop had not been forecasted in time, and it was well inside the product and material lead times needed to secure parts and manufacture the product. That led to a mad scramble to fill sales orders. Already putting in incredibly long hours, we worked even longer to figure out how to do so, looking at all avenues from hand carrying material on airplanes to quality reworks. We drove our suppliers as hard as we could and left no stone unturned. If we could not ship in time for the holiday season, we knew the orders would disappear.

As a result, allocation fights broke out among the sales teams and our customers. In typical fashion, the Supply Chain took the brunt of the blame. Despite all the herculean efforts, we did not come close to fulfilling the order book. Orders got cancelled, and customers became extremely upset. They had invested in this product for their holiday season promotions, yet they constantly were stocked out. We also incurred huge supplier liability for product we no longer had demand for and were hit with significant expedited freight costs. This truly was a disaster. We failed!

But did we?

A couple of weeks into the next fiscal quarter, we put all our efforts into cleaning up the mess we had made. Morale was extremely low. No bonuses were coming, but the next round of layoffs was imminent. This was a bitter cold January morning—and one of the most disturbing moments of my career. As I passed the security desk and walked into the office building, I could not believe my eyes. There were posters hung up everywhere exclaiming:

Congratulations to the Supply Chain!

We achieved the highest Inventory Turns in the history of the company!

("Inventory turns" is a ratio showing how many times a company has sold and replaced inventory during a given period. The higher the turns, the better the cash flow.)

Speechless, I stood in amazement that someone would have the audacity to promote himself/herself when the company was in a tailspin. Obviously, the Supply Chain leader was doing this solely for self-preservation purposes. With our one mainstream product, we sold everything that we had, but we did not come close to meeting the sales orders placed. As a result, we severely missed the earnings forecast.

Really? We are patting ourselves on the back when we failed? Thank goodness someone had the sense to take down the signs later that day, but the damage had already been done.

That morning forever changed me. My takeaway was that the Supply Chain leader was measured only on a few key metrics, one of them being inventory turns, despite the business outcome. I vowed that if I ever became a senior executive, I would do whatever I could to balance the metrics, measures, and goals among revenue, costs, and cash flow. "We would never celebrate achieving only one metric."

We would never celebrate achieving only one metric

Taking this to heart proved to be one of best yet most challenging choices I have ever made.

I've realized that many consultants love to tout "best in class metrics" in isolation but fail to bring in the value of how they interact with one another. Never will I strive to achieve any single "best-in-class" key metric (except forecast accuracy) because they need to *complement* one another, not *compete against* each other. Customer satisfaction, revenue, costs, and trade working capital need to balance.

During my journey, I have experienced much success with many failures. As I continue to learn and refine, I ask, "Do any key performance metrics drive direct or indirect biases in our demand forecast? Do some of our key metrics hold more weight than others?" To answer that, I put together a qualitative assessment and hypothesized how the metric, or lack thereof, would influence each organization on how it would influence demand forecast biases (being either high or low bias). After putting the initial list together, I discussed with other functions what key performance indicators (KPIs) were in each of their goals. See Figure 2 for the results. (If no goals were set for the function, I still classified many of them as contributing to forecast bias since it was a goal they would not be measured on and would not have to worry about.)

Key Performance Indicator (KPI)	Function/Demand Bias							
	Sales	Engineering	Product	Quality	Finance	Procurement	Operations	Planning
On-Time Delivery	High		High	High			High	High
Inventory Turns	High	High	High		Low		Low	Low
Demand Forecast Accuracy	High	High	High	High			Low	Low
Excess and Obsolescence	High	High	High		Low		Low	Low
Revenue Attainment	High	High	High	High	High	High	High	High
Product Cost		High	High		High	High	Low	Low
Overall Demand Bias	**High**	**High**	**High**	**High**	**Neutral**	**High**	**Low**	**Low**

No Goals Set for Function

Figure 2

The results were not at all surprising. After all the hyperbole in our S&OP process in aligning our KPIs, the actual KPIs that hit the function's measures were non-existent. This helped explain why we tended to *over-forecast* most of the demand.

From a Sales point of view, the only thing that drove every salesperson I spoke with was hitting revenue goals. Commissions and incentives were set solely on those goals. Although they acknowledge cost as a factor, achieving revenue was their top priority. Furthermore, most of salespeople said the revenue targets set upon them were not achievable. They felt pressured to drive a demand plan that not only covered the revenue but would drive plenty of inventory on each product, giving them flexibility to develop promotions that could increase the volume at a moment's notice. Most felt they needed this flexibility to respond to customers or block competitors when the need arose.

There was also pressure on salespeople from individual Product Managers who tried to influence them to forecast his/her product. When asked about forecast accuracy measures, most did not understand how they were calculated, saying that calculation was only important for Supply Chain and Operations.

Speaking with Engineering proved interesting. I understood the function was not directly involved in the sales and operations planning process—nor did they care about it. However, Engineering had a significant effect on the forecast bias. Its primary input to the process was hitting new product launch dates. Despite all the measures, gates, and program management processes to determine product readiness,

Engineering would not come off the initial launch date until the last minute when there was no chance of gaining product acceptance. From here, the product launch would move out 45 to 60 days, only to repeat this cycle several times until it launched 8 to 12 months later than originally planned. This was one of the key contributors that hurt forecast accuracy and added costs to the existing product portfolio. *Clearly, product transitions were not planned properly.*

I found forecasting with the Product Management team fascinating because forecasting bias was highly prominent. Each manager would forecast his/her product in isolation. Once I added the entire forecast by the Product Management team, the numbers would be *three times* what we could ever achieve in sales. One of my dearest colleagues called this the "parenting effect." Imagine the product manager judging a beauty contest that his/her child was in. Obviously, bias would be present.

Also, a contentious area with Product Management was how much volume to forecast for a new product at its launch. The push from Product Management was to forecast the volumes stated in the business case because that's how the cost and revenue was determined to approve funding of the program. Unfortunately, market conditions changed, and the product launch dates were significantly pushed out, nullifying the original business case. "However, these volumes still had to be in forecast." This was another key area of forecast bias that added significant costs.

The Quality team also had an influence on the demand forecast. They would pick key measures and put improvement goals around them. Outside of actual product quality issues, they would also add customer-facing metrics. The key quantitative measure was on-time delivery, and we consistently failed to achieve it. We would create cross-functional tasks forces led by a six sigma "black belt" to work on improving on-time delivery. But success or failure correlated to how good or poor our forecast accuracy was—mostly poor. We would then drive another task force to improve forecast accuracy. This ended up going through all the heuristics on why the forecast accuracy was so poor. It concluded we needed to change talent and "forecast more" to improve on-time delivery.

It was also generalized that "Sales needs to forecast better." (I expound on this dangerous mindset in the next chapter.)

Tackling the root causes of product launch timing, aligning cross-functional metrics and goals, and product quality issues never came together in this company. Nothing significantly or sustainably improved in on-time delivery. We had put a significant amount of time, effort, and cost to drive improvements that never transpired.

Our Finance team was one of the key voices of reason in the S&OP process, but its members did not hold much clout. When we rolled up the pre-consensus product forecasts, Finance team members would run the financials and state the obvious: "The forecast was too high." But the team was viewed as having limited understanding of the market and the company's product portfolio, so the inputs were easily dismissed. I nicknamed the Finance people the "I told you so" team. That is because at the end of every earnings cycle when financial guidance or trade working capital goals were missed, we would hear that phrase from them.

Our Procurement team also added bias to the demand forecast. To achieve product cost targets, many suppliers would be signed up to volume-tiered pricing, sometimes in the form of a rebate or new pricing once hitting a certain volume threshold. These negotiations were baselined from a previous demand forecast (full of bias) and sometimes with an estimated stretch of volume to hit a price that would include buying inventory if the volumes were not met. This resulted from the one and only key metric the Procurement team was measured on—material purchase price.

As time went on and the demand signals changed, it would become obvious we would not come close to meeting our volume agreements. The Purchasing team would jump in and tell the supplier the volumes would increase in the next cycle. Then they would bring this input into the next demand forecasting cycle. This would influence the demand forecast, ending in additional inventory-carrying and obsolescence costs. Over time, I have coined this phenomenon as "lowest price does not mean lowest cost." Quality, liability, suppler reliability, lead-times, landed cost, and payment terms should all be factored into the lowest cost equation—a concept many leaders struggle to grasp.

> *Quality, liability, supplier reliability, lead-times, landed cost, and payment terms should all be factored into the lowest cost equation—a concept many leaders struggle to grasp.*

Organizationally, structuring in a dedicated Customer Operations team did have a positive effect on forecast bias. Bringing in new variables including peer-to-peer customer operations forecasts, customer inventory visibility and sales, and balanced metrics did help remove a part of the bias. This was the only team (besides Planning) that had a forecast accuracy metric in their individual goals. This did improve our forecast accuracy, which ended up plateauing. The Operations team still had to forecast the planned new product launch dates and were heavily influenced to tie them to the revenue targets the Sales Management team signed up to. In turn, these two key influencers drove the bias in Operations.

Planning was the only area to be measured on-time delivery, revenue attainment, and trade working capital. This did help drive the analysis on where forecast inputs did not make sense, but much bias still prevailed. A key driver was to submit a demand forecast that met the revenue targets and still have the correct amount and mix of inventory to improve on-time deliveries. In this case, we would bias the demand forecast on the higher end, but low enough where we had a chance of meeting inventory targets by the end of the fiscal period.

Another bias clearly surfaced for me—developing a demand forecast that avoided as much internal organizational conflict as possible. This was especially sensitive around new product introduction dates and hitting revenue targets set by the Sales VPs. In this position, I felt I wore a target on my back if my team did not provide forecast input that hit the revenue line. We feared calling out individual "senior executives" for massaging revenue plans based on unrealistic agendas.

In managing the S&OP process, I knew we had to do something differently. Out of self-defense, I changed our demand meetings in which the Operations team members had to explain their individual forecasts for our key large customers. My team and I would analyze their forecast, prepare slides to ask questions on each key customer, and the Operations team would defend the forecast. This approach was designed to deflect some of the possible conflict. If the Operations person could not justify the forecast submitted, it would be changed when we drove the new demand signal. (Setting this up showed how much influence the organization's "politics" had on our forecast.)

My experiences at this time shaped how I began to modify my own behaviors, achieve better balance measures and metrics, and improve my political clout. The goal: to improve the forecasting accuracy.

Not all companies have the same organizational structure. Depending on your organization, Marketing, Human Resources, IT, Legal, or others can influence the planning. As long as human beings are involved, biases will always exist in the forecast. The key is making sure the process weeds out *extreme* biases that could hurt the overall business.

I have found success with two key organizational elements: (1) Nurturing the best culture to operate in and (2) having the correct leader. This leader has the final say in the demand forecast and grasps the delicate, uncertain balance among customer satisfaction, revenue, cost, and trade working capital. These elements need to be able to work together to have success.

Yes, achieving this is easier said than done. But I have seen it work extremely well when both elements exist in a collaborative way.

Chapter 6:
Forecasting Myths

Demand forecasting, by its very nature, is extremely complex. Many companies spend countless hours and dollars on task forces, tools, and systems to improve the demand forecast. Often, the results of these investments are bitterly disappointing. Why is this? Is it because we do not have the right process, people, systems, and/or tools? These could be part of the problem, but certain widely held beliefs inside organizations exist—ones I have found to be mostly mythical. Yet, if these myths are not addressed, they will hamper any sustainable improvement and drive bias in the demand forecast.

Do you or leaders in your organization believe the following to be true?

1. The sales team knows what to forecast and just needs to apply more effort.

2. Customers know what they want.

3. Forecast accuracy is better at other companies.

4. Your organization's metrics and goals are balanced.

5. Achieving "consensus" in the demand forecast results in the most accurate forecast.

6. "Leadership" understands potential consequences of the demand forecast.

7. Investing in Artificial Intelligence (AI) will significantly improve the demand forecast.

MYTH 1: The Sales team knows what to forecast and just needs to apply more effort.

The exclamation "Sales needs to be held accountable for the forecast" probably resonates at least once a day in many businesses. The frustration of driving too much or little capacity, filling non-forecasted sales orders, and having aged inventory all lead to when the item was forecasted—either that, or it was nowhere on the radar. There may be some truth that the effort put forth in creating a Sales forecast could be better. But I have experienced that investing in resources and tools to improve the Sales team's forecast rarely yield substantial improvements. To me, "holding salespeople accountable" is a dangerous statement that not only drives organizational barriers and discord but holds no value to achieving business results. Depending on the size of your organization, Sales could involve hundreds or thousands of people. Do you hold every single person responsible for each individual forecast?

What if the simple answer was "the salesperson just doesn't know?" Depending on the customer and/or industry, many variables influencing sales are simply unknown and realistically cannot be captured. An accurate forecast needs to articulate what, when, and where, yet the information behind this might not be readily available. Factors such as competition, competing internal priorities, relationships, organizational changes, historical behaviors, quality perceptions, geo-political, product/solution testing, and weather are just a few that can affect actual sales orders.

Finding an answer in holding salespeople accountable for forecasting may simply be wasted effort. In my experience, the Sales forecasts make a good starting point, but when all forecasts are aggregated, many other variables must be analyzed to drive a more accurate demand forecast. Getting past this mindset is crucial in to provide focus on other factors/ inputs to achieve better results.

MYTH 2: Customers know what they want.

Some believe the Customer has the best input to creating an accurate forecast. Nothing could be further from the truth! Unless Customers have "skin in the game" (meaning they signed up for a form of financial liability), their forecasts are typically poor.

Also, in most cases, a "Customer" is not a single entity but are many people with competing agendas and information. The spokesperson for "Customers" is probably not aware of all the relevant variables and has different assumptions about the forecast than others in their organization. This myth needs to be viewed for what it is.

However, there are investments that can be made with key customers to help the company's short-term planning and replenishment process. A formal and disciplined Collaborative Planning, Forecasting, and Replenishment (CPFR) process can improve the near term forecast as well as revenue, costs, and trade working capital for both organizations. This process develops a cadence in which inventory, sell through, sales orders, marketing plans, and inventory are transparently shared between organizations and results measured. The process can bring earlier visibility to sales orders, align the demand forecast, and lead to improved business results. In a competitive replenishment environment, implementing this process helped my company "out-supply chain" our competitors. By itself, this brought in more business for us and drove better revenue and margins.

Investing in CPFR process is not for every organization, but it could be considered, depending on the industry and channel.

MYTH 3: Forecast accuracy is much better at other companies.

I have yet to meet Supply Chain people anywhere in the world who say the forecast accuracy they rely upon is any good. External Supply Chain consultants feast on this when they present their findings to the executive staff. I call this approach "preying upon a company's inferiority complex." Beware, consultants love to compare the forecast accuracy measured in the organization to "best-in-class metrics" experienced elsewhere. This is an area where most executives lack experience asking relevant questions. In working with consultants during my tenure, I never got a straight answer on these questions when making the forecast accuracy comparisons:

- ☑ Is this measurement compared to a competitor or someone in the same industry?
- ☑ How is the "best in class" forecast accuracy measured? Is the comparison you are making "apples to apples"?
- ☑ How many SKUs (products) make up the "best in class" forecast?
- ☑ What is the sales order lead time this "best in class" company requires to fulfill an order?
- ☑ Is the "best in class" forecast accuracy one data point or an average?
- ☑ Over what time periods is accuracy being measured?

Typically, questions such of these are not asked with the assumption that the comparisons are "apples to apples." I have yet to work with any organization in which demand forecast accuracy consistently exceeded 40% compared with the prior month forecast mix accuracy using a mean-weighted average calculation by SKU.

Understanding your forecast accuracy measurements and constantly analyzing actual sales orders for improvements should be key to developing and refining your organization's supply chain strategy.

MYTH 4: Your organization's metrics and goals are balanced.

In many organizations, typically quantitative goals set forth are cascaded to many functions of the organization. These can include revenue, margin, inventory turns, inventory reserves, on-time delivery, and forecast accuracy. Outside of forecast accuracy, the rest of these metrics can compete with one another. For instance, to hit on-time delivery measures, there is a natural push to hold more inventory to manage uncertainty. In this way, inventory turns are negatively affected. The margin can be based on the revenue and product mix forecast; however, if the volume is lower than forecast, it could affect the margin, given capacities are under-utilized and supplier volume pricing agreements are not met. The trade-off could be building more inventory to compensate, but this could be risky in the long term. It could even signal an unhealthy balance sheet during the earnings period and increase inventory risk leading to stock price erosion.

I have found that organizations look at these key metrics in isolation and neglect to assign someone to orchestrate the balance, instead they have people and organizations "fight it out." Each metric's goal is set on historical measures, and a continuous improvement percentage is applied to it. By the very nature and formulation of the goal, a metric by itself might be achievable but rarely metrics are all achieved consistently. Why? It is because of the way goals are set and managed independently within different functions of the organization. In a simplistic sense, Sales has revenue goals tied to sales while Supply Chain goals are tied to cost, on-time delivery, inventory turns, and inventory reserves. This causes natural tension between the two groups. Thus, often, decisions are made to hit the metric but miss the bigger picture—potential risks to the company and/or customer. By recognizing this, goals can be set up to be better balanced.

At supply chain seminars, I often hear speakers tout their companies' on-time delivery, declaring it to be consistently at or near 100%. On-time delivery is perceived as a great measure to equate to customer satisfaction. But that might be a myth in itself!

I am always skeptical of reporting consistently high numbers for on-time delivery measures. Many times, internal measures for delivery may not equate to customer satisfaction or even be competitive. For instance, organizations can set up sales order lead times that, if shipped on or prior to the lead time, equals success. Many times, these lead times are not well-orchestrated, and the actual customer ordering may not know, understand, nor care that these lead times are established. However, supply chain personnel go to great lengths to make sure they can hit the on-time delivery metric—one that can include expediting costs while sacrificing existing sales orders and forecasts and adding inventories that put pressure on hitting other key measures.

Being accountable for S&OP for a long time, I have joked with executive teams saying, "If I have done my job, I will piss off each of your functions equally." That means I will not focus on achieving any one specific metric. Rather, I strive to make the best decision to "de-risk" a poor outcome. This is where "art" outweighs the "science" in the S&OP process.

Perceived as having a balanced view of the metrics, a good grasp on the business impacts, and understanding tradeoffs and potential consequences has enabled my team and I to earn a high degree of trust. For decisions that were significant, driving alignment within the organization was critical. For example, I would sacrifice hitting an on-time delivery date compared with adding incremental expediting costs if the customer had ample inventory and shipping the order was not necessary for the fiscal period. This takes a high degree of visibility, collaboration, alignment, and most important, trust.

MYTH 5: Achieving "consensus" in the demand forecast is the best forecast.

In traditional S&OP practices, a formal review of demand signal occurs in which inputs are analyzed and multiple functions align on the demand forecast. This process is called Consensus Demand. In theory, this means having multiple points of view and information, then collectively leveraging them to create a uniform demand signal versus being managed in isolation. Putting this process into practice has been an evolution.

Many organizations that have implemented a formal S&OP process struggle with developing a meaningful "consensus" demand. A consensus meeting usually takes place at the mid-management level of an organization and can quickly become ineffective. For example, it could be dominated by someone with a persuasive agenda. It could lack priorities on what to cover, for the prescribed meeting templates are too complex and/or confusing. It could easily be a check-to-box review filled with apathy and poor attendance.

How could this be? Doesn't the demand signal drive every tangible operational decision in creating/modifying purchase orders, capacity decisions, inventory reserves, and future investments? Why would organizations become somewhat apathetic to this process when it so important? The answers come down to organizational clarity, time and practicality, individual incentives, and of course, individual perceptions.

Have you ever asked the question "who is responsible for demand forecast?" Often, you will hear the names of functions: Sales, Supply Chain, Operations, Product Management, or even the "system." Now ask "what individual in your company is ultimately responsible for the demand forecast?" The answers range from "well, we hold this consensus meeting" to "the CEO is ultimately responsible." As you can see, either the question is not really answered, or accountability is just assumed.

If your organization cannot answer these questions, you are not alone. Having someone responsible for the final demand forecast is something to consider. As expressed earlier, *a highly emotional, intelligent person who has a good grasp on the market and supply chain coupled with a senior level role can drive improvement while removing bias from the forecast.* Even though the experience may be like finding a leprechaun, this kind of person does exist and/or can be developed. For example, how many companies have a VP of Planning? Even though this may be a considerable investment, the actual return on investment can be enormous. Having someone with the mindset of being accountable for an accurate demand forecast is a game-changer.

MYTH 6: "Leadership" understands the potential consequences of the demand forecast.

One of my favorite myths is believing that "leadership" fully understands the consequences of decisions made. Yes, a leader might be well-versed in one area, but in other areas, the experience of a leader when connecting a decision to specific consequence might not resonate. How many times have you heard "well, (insert executive name) is aware and agreed with the decision"? Throwing weight behind names of executives can be dangerous depending on the situation. When it comes to what and how much to forecast, tiebreakers sought from a senior leader on what to forecast can be done in isolation when the person seeking direction does not disclose or even understand the consequences himself/herself.

Taking this a step further, some senior leaders may be inundated with requests for approvals because the existing process demands it. Being in a similar situation myself, it would be impossible to fully understand the potential consequences of every decision I faced. I had to trust my team members that their request for approval was fully vetted before reaching my approval status. It is easy to assume that, since I approved a request, I really understood the potential consequences. Sadly, I did not.

This myth is a trap many organizations fall into. If it is perceived that someone is to blame, it will justify the decision so the process can move on. Indeed, many leaders may not know their names were used for justification nor readily understand the potential effect. When confronted with the decision, experienced leaders should ask probing questions about alternatives and possible consequences to the alternatives. He/she may be surprised to learn answers to questions may not be well thought through, given an urgent need to move the S&OP process along and meet deadlines. Leaders must be conscious of this trap and avoid it as much as possible.

MYTH 7: Investing in Artificial Intelligence (AI) will significantly improve the demand forecast.

I consider trusting Artificial Intelligence (AI) to improve the demand signal a myth (at the time of writing). Using disparate information from customers, distribution channels, suppliers, and organizational data can trigger early visibility on product replenishment, but this is near-term phenomena. The amount of data accuracy and organization around AI is enormous. So far, current investments made in AI for forecasting have shown underwhelming results. As far as I know, human beings do not always make rational decisions, so I struggle on how AI can predict that! However, I believe there is a place for AI, especially in product replenishment, but it will take a lot of time and data to accurately predict human decisions and the chain of reactions they might take.

When investing in any new tools and technology, I like to ask, "What are the problems we are trying to solve and how will this tool improve our company's financial results?" It is amazing to see various and vague "leap of faith" answers I get from internal stakeholders about the benefits. Going into any project, the goal should be to pursue a clear and measurable financial benefit that correlates to the investment made. Many business cases manufacture an answer, but often, they are bullish on results and rarely achieve the desired outcome. Clearly articulating in the business case, the issue(s) attempting to be solved and what benefits the investment will provide, should help. Stating a range of benefits would be more realistic since the investment itself is not a standalone. People, processes, and data management need to be addressed, which should not be underestimated when discussing an investment in tools or technologies.

These myths are based on my personal experience. I have found that many companies subscribe to some or all of them, sometimes unconsciously. What forecasting myths reside within your organization? Step back and put your own list together, then share it with collective stakeholders and get their feedback. If an honest discussion can be had, a new shared set of assumptions can emerge. They can curb cross-functional animosities and put focus on driving overall forecast improvement.

Chapter 7:
Strive for Inventory Visibility

"Our supply chain is weak" was the clear message I received from many employees when I joined an established company to lead the Planning function. "We always have too much inventory of the wrong product and we never have the right product to fulfill sales orders on time." There was a lot of functional friction within the company, even though a basic S&OP process was established, and a standardized Enterprise Resource Planning (ERP) system had just been implemented. I heard our CEO say he despised traveling due to all the Sales team and customer complaints he heard on not having product readily available when they needed it.

Even though all employees had the same logo on their name badges, an "us versus them" mentality prevailed. "Now, the next know-it-all"—me— "will come in and say all the right things. But he too will fail, just like the long legacy of Planning leaders did." This was a great challenge for me—that is, to leverage a new team as well as my experience and interpersonal skills to accomplish something different for the company.

First, I sought to understand the entire supply chain, end to end, (from customer to supplier) and try to understand the value each node in the supply chain brought. Through this analysis, quite a few process "disconnects" were discovered. With a few tweaks and better alignment among the processes, I believed a small investment in reporting and modification in organizational responsibilities could pay big dividends. Here were some the challenges our organization was facing:

- ☑ Sales and shipments were heavily back-end loaded for the fiscal quarter, driving uneven capacity in our distribution centers. The last few days of the fiscal quarter resembled a mad scramble.
- ☑ We had a 2- to 4-day sales order to ship lead time SLA with all customers.
- ☑ We had a comprehensive rebate agreement with our Distributor customers (the bulk of our revenue) that allowed a generous return privileges, which was highly leveraged.
- ☑ Product costs ended higher than planned because of end-of-quarter expedited transportation to fulfill sales orders.
- ☑ We would continually show "red" on all the key metrics for forecast accuracy, on-time delivery, inventory turns, transportation costs, and inventory obsolesce costs.
- ☑ We saw a lot of "cover your ass" work at the beginning of the quarter on why sales orders were not shipped at the end of the quarter.

The good news? We had a relatively strong company culture (especially in our C-suite) of admitting uncertainty in how to improve. They agreed to let the experts come in and trusted in our recommended process improvements. Remarkably, our company had a comprehensive view of our distributor inventory and their sales which was only being leveraged for financial reasons. Knowing this was invaluable to me.

What surprised me was that sales from our distributor partners to customers were evenly shipped throughout the fiscal quarter. Yet, we shipped most of the orders to the distribution partners at the end of the fiscal period. That meant we had a "win-win" opportunity with our distribution partners. With a little teamwork, this collaboration would improve the overall costs and cash flows for both organizations.

What else? We needed to include a couple more elements in our distributor agreements. We agreed on monthly sales order volume percentages to prevent back-end loading of orders. To better manage inventories and cash flow, we also developed inventory boundaries (a range of "weeks on hand" inventory) that the distributor would be responsible to carry. Adding inventory boundaries would prevent stuffing the channel with inventory or having too little inventory in the channel.

Due to good reporting and analytics, we saw big improvements quickly, including our shipments becoming more level-loaded throughout the fiscal period, all but eliminating overtime costs at the end of the quarter. In addition, new sales orders could be challenged and analyzed if the distributor already had too much inventory on hand. Consequently, product returns from the distributor were cut more than half. Also, order suggestions were made to the distributor when their inventory levels were too low for a specific SKU. Our expedite costs dropped significantly because we had a better understanding if the distributor was at risk of stocking out with our non-expedited delivery date. Both the distributors and our company saved significant costs on shipping, labor, and returns while improving cash flows on both sides. Product availability issues all but disappeared.

As stated, our metrics for on-time shipping did not improve much. That is because more information was available to determine if a product needed to be expedited or not for risk of running out of inventory at the point of distribution. In a lot of cases, we would forego on-time shipping versus expedited costs—that is, if we could still achieve the revenue target for the fiscal period and not stock out the distributor.

About a year into this new role, I noticed quite a bit of change. The squabbling between functions was muted, our business results improved, our distributors rarely had shortages issues (thus eventually increasing revenue), our orders and shipments were level loaded throughout the quarter, and product returns were cut in half. The CEO even confided in me that he enjoyed traveling again because he rarely got the complaints, he once did on product availability. What's more, revenue, costs, and trade working capital all improved.

To accomplish all this took an individual with experience who created a vision and plan, assumed the lead, facilitated collaboration across functional organizations, and make necessary changes to achieve better results.

Despite initial skepticism, at the base of this change was the overall company culture, which was the key enabler that could foster this change.

I have found that an organization's focus on long-term decision making is usually usurped by the "fire drill of the day" (dealing with short-term issues). This can become another vicious circle. Failure to thoughtfully plan and forecast will keep driving short-term issues. What happens? Supply chains worldwide create heroes—the "firefighters" who extinguish the blaze and then fight the next one.

Over my career, I became an expert firefighter, being called in to fight immense infernos. Even though I felt satisfaction when the blaze was out, I always got caught up in the forensics that reported the root cause of the fire. Many of the outcomes pointed toward poor planning. As the company's lead for Planning, I was put in a defensive position.

Over time, I held on to those forensics and made fresh discoveries. For example, product that was expedited for a sale to a distributor was eventually returned because it had too much stock. Knowing the amount of inventory the distributor was sitting on at the time of the order would have changed the decision to add expediting costs and/or question if the product was even needed.

Another example was our Product team demanding to have a certain number of units at the launch of the product, only for it to sit in inventory for several months before gaining any traction. Many times, the product got reworked or scrapped because of initial quality and/or design changes. Meanwhile, our salespeople could be commissioned on a distributor sale they were never aware of nor even involved with. Also, multiple salespeople could receive commission on the same sale. This made it quite challenging for Sales to provide a comprehensive input into the demand forecast.

While I could have easily fallen into the trap of pointing out these revelations and blaming others, doing so would not bode well since I wanted to drive a collaborative culture. Why trigger a lose-lose situation and be part of the blame game?

Why trigger a lose-lose situation and become part of the blame game?

Instead of fighting "fire with fire" (no pun intended), I wondered how I could obtain more facts and become more knowledgeable. Then we could make more informed decisions before driving up costs with no recognizable end-value. Instead of firefighters, what if we developed a team of "Smokey Bears" who could *prevent* hazards before they could ever be set ablaze? I know we could not eliminate *all* fires, but if we could *reduce* them, we could be more proactive than reactive. That would save us a lot in costs while dealing with less turmoil.

In the industries and go-to market channels I was involved in, gaining broader visibility on inventories and sales was monumental. My goal was to break the traditional organizational myths explained in Chapter 6. By gaining channel inventory visibility while developing the proper reporting, metrics, and analysis, the Supply Chain would be able to better anticipate orders as well as challenge the orders that did not make sense.

Gaining supplier inventory visibility completed the equation. Understanding key supplier inventories and "real" lead times helped us decide when we needed to pull triggers before adding costs in expedites. Visibility aided in gaining understanding of our contracted liability when we would not consume the supplier liability caused by our forecast to them. This helped us mitigate liabilities before it was too late. Gaining visibility to channel and supplier inventory proved to be invaluable and more influential than I ever imagined.

> *Gaining visibility to channel and supplier inventory proved to be invaluable and more influential than I ever imagined.*

Investing in securing customer, channel, and supplier inventory visibility with the proper reporting, metrics, and decision criteria can be transformational. Realistically, this information will not be perfect, but it can provide directional insights and enable organizations to become proactive rather than reactive. This kind of investment reduces the amount of firefighting needed and brings in more data to assist in the forecasting process to battle forecast bias.

Chapter 8:
Lead Time Decision-Making

We had a solid product with good margins and high volume of sales. The quality was also high, and it performed well in the market. This scenario was becoming scarcer for us as time went on. This product, however, was powered by an older chipset that would soon be discontinued and no longer manufactured by our supplier. It was "last call" for orders from the supplier who would build and ship the chips in four months' time. No worries, based on our latest forecast, we did not need to order any more chipsets because a new product with the latest chip technology was forthcoming. The new product—to be launched in three months—was the replacement for the existing product. Therefore, we had enough chipset supply secured to build the remainder of the existing product's forecast. All would be fine . . . or would it?

What if the new product fell into the same issues as previous new product launches? What if the schedule continually slipped when we got to the final network testing stage like all its predecessors? As leaders of our S&OP processes, we performed numerous analyses on new product launches. From them, we noted a trend that, when we started testing at the final network testing stage, new issues would keep coming up, causing us to delay the launch an average of six months. If this happened again, do we just accept this reality and have a gap in the portfolio, missing the current product's revenue and margin? It would be too late in the process to keep our current product alive. Here was my thinking. If I followed the S&OP process by the book and took the new product launch date as being precise, we would be fine. After all, if the product timeline did slip and we could not build any more of the current product, at least I had somewhere to push the blame. Besides, if I challenged the projected launch timeline, I would have to go through all the political hurdles to call out this risk. It would challenge the new Technology Manager who had insisted the product would ship on time. The Technology Manager was highly emotional and well-connected among the senior leaders in the organization. He would drag my reputation through the mud if I did this. I should just "stay in my lane" and follow all the posted traffic signals. I had to carefully think through this: to challenge or not to challenge this Technology Leader and, by extension, the senior executives who supported him.

I had a young family to care for. Getting fired for political reasons would be financially detrimental to me—not counting the big hit to my self-esteem and perceived worth. Just leave this alone. But knowing what would likely happen, I could not turn my back on this issue. I was tired of being "bullied" into decisions that were political in nature and detrimental to the outcome for our company. Plus, this was happening as we continued to walk co-workers (and my friends) out the door due to organizational downsizing. Heck, if I got fired, at least I could hold my head high, knowing I tried to do the right thing.

Given these circumstances, I held a private meeting that included the Technology Leader, the General Manager of the region, and the VP of Finance. I understood that, this particular region would be greatly affected financially by a delay in the new product launch. I recommended we invest in an insurance policy to purchase more chipsets if the new product was delayed. I presented the data and facts from previously product launches. The data outlined reasons for those delays and what it would mean to our revenue margin if this tier of product were missing from our portfolio for a period of time. What happened? The Technology Manager vehemently argued that the new product would be launched on time. He even said I was wasting his time having this meeting (a theme I have heard several times in my career). But surprisingly, the Region General Manager and the Finance VP agreed with my recommendation, reinforcing the need to put in place an insurance policy. They decided the company would assume a four-month delay in the new product launch and purchase the appropriate material and chipsets to cover this period. Upon hearing this, the Technology Manager was visibility upset and exhibited behaviors of a person who felt his integrity was being challenged. As we walked out the meeting room together, the Technology Manager scolded me. He said I had no right to challenge his authority and that he knew what he was doing. Refusing to hear my rebuttal, he stormed off.

A couple of days later, one of our engineers called me. He stated that the Technology Manager told the Engineering Team I did not believe in their work. I think he said this to motivate the engineers to prove me wrong and allow him to save face. The engineer said the adjectives about me coming out of the manager's mouth would make a sailor blush. He adamantly told them it is their job to "shove all the excess supply of the current product up my butt" (or something to that effect). He affirmed that they will meet the current schedule, and therefore we did not need an insurance policy. This did not surprise me, but it told me I should go and see the Technology Manager to try and make peace.

When I arrived at his office, the door was open, as he sat behind his desk. As I walked in, I noticed a dartboard with my photo on it from the corner of my eye. His bullying and intimidation practices were in full swing. So, I picked up the darts and started throwing them at the dartboard. Then I told him he had every right to feel angry with me. In fact, he should mass produce the dartboard for he could sell a lot of them. Not in the mood for joking, he sternly asked me to leave. As the months passed, it turned out some of the existing product had to be "stuffed up my butt" but only a small fraction of excess. The new product was officially delayed thirty days before the planned launch date with multiple delays following that date.

Finally, it did launch—five months later than originally planned. Fortunately, the margin made by extending the life of the existing product far outweighed any consequences of the small leftover obsolescence costs. Our company experienced a better business outcome because we did not ignore the facts and blame another group for a failure.

At the time, I thought my actions might end my career with this company. Sticking my neck out did ruffle many feathers. But at the same time, I left others extremely impressed, especially our VP of Procurement. He told me this was the first time in a while that someone courageously stood up to the "new product introduction politics" and made a sound business decision. It was clear this would become an issue even with all the commitments and promises made for the new product. But I was able to leverage my previous technology experience and data analysis to help change the outcome. At the end of the day, we prevented a major fire. We tackled the politics head-on by presenting data analytics in a fashion that affected the outcome. This was my first real experience in raising a longer-term issue and adjusting course at the proper time. Previously, I kept getting caught up in the fire of the day, preventing all of us from focusing on the future. How could we take this experience and apply it more broadly, so it would be easier to uncover issues and make better decisions before it's too late?

> *"Never make a decision too early, but*
> *never make a decision when it's too*
> *late." — a wise manager*

A wise manager once told me, "Never make a decision too early, but never make a decision when it's too late." This advice stuck with me. I knew there would be no better place to apply this guidance than managing S&OP. We had spent countless hours arguing over forecasts that ended up significantly changing the next cycle but had little or no effect on business results. We also had failed to put enough focus on product transitions and/or we started end-of-life planning scenarios too late in the process. Instead, we found ourselves firefighting, chasing critical parts, or trying to find homes for excess inventories and supplier liabilities. So, I thought, "What if we put together a set of 'rules of thumb' to help identify problems and make decisions by weighing the costs of deciding too early versus too late?" Through much collaboration, we developed a chart (Figure 3) that focused our energies on when to make key decisions. Figure 3 Though relatively simple to put together, the chart's effectiveness proved to be substantial. Using this lens on a particular product category's forecast helped us determine what demand decisions we needed to make based on lead times. It also made us ask better questions, streamline our meetings, and prioritize where we spend time on critical decisions. If if we made decisions inside lead times, it would cost us more in the end.

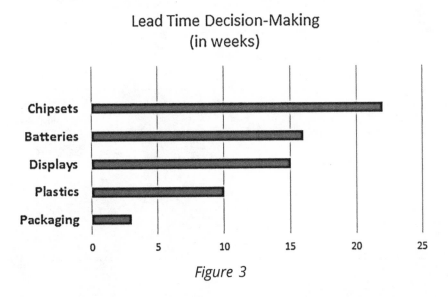

Figure 3

Yes, there were still politics involved in making decisions. But by putting focus and effort on when we needed to decide, we took a lot of noise out of the forecast process and we were able to focus on key topics only. As a result, we reduced the number of near-term fires and operational costs were reduced. Does your organization tend to manage mostly short-term issues and continually put out fires? If so, you are not alone. No matter how well an organization plans, the realities will always present challenges. But consider how many of your short-term issues were self-induced inside the four walls of your company? I would estimate over half of them came from some type of organizational disconnect, poor communication, or planning with a political bias that never came to fruition. For us, putting together the lead time decision criteria had proven to be extremely beneficial in focusing on "something" rather than "everything" while curbing the number of fires that flared. Do you manage decisions around critical lead times within your company? If not, it could prove very beneficial.

Chapter 9:
Characteristics of an S&OP Lead

While interviewing for a position at one company, I spoke with their current S&OP lead. I knew that if I got hired, responsibility for this position would shift to me, and he could not wait to get rid of it! The interview quickly turned into a therapy session. The interviewer barely covered any of my qualifications. Rather, he focused on issues with the company's S&OP process and quickly went into a diatribe about the poor support by its key players. He stated how the consensus demand meetings were dominated by the product team and the demand planners were, basically, pushovers. He said the company was following the prescribed process to the "t," but meetings were viewed as a waste of time.

He ran the monthly executive meeting, which was attended by the entire senior staff. But he struggled to get engagement or bring up uncomfortable issues. When I asked about the make-up of his organization, he said he had only two analysts reporting to him and Planning was in a different management structure.

I thought the interviewer would have a nervous breakdown; he was so tense. But I assured him I brought a lot of experience in this area—not only in the process itself, but in managing the entire organization through the process. After the conversation, I felt energized that, with a culture willing to change coupled with my willingness to listen and learn, this could be an excellent challenge. I would be a good fit.

A few days later, the hiring manager offered me the position to lead Global Planning. I graciously asked if it was okay to speak with the Chief Operation Officer (COO), Chief Financial Officer (CFO), and Senior Vice President of Sales. I explained I would be a good fit if the company allowed me to operate and collaborate outside of Supply Chain. Being "boxed in" the Supply Chain area and "do what I was told" would limit my understanding what challenges the organization faced cross-functionally. He agreed, and I had discussions with the three leaders.

Particularly encouraging was hearing all three leaders express these main points:

▸ We do not have experience in the S&OP arena.
▸ We need someone to coordinate cross-functionally.
▸ We have customer satisfaction, cost, and working capital opportunities we need to improve.

Basically, I received the same answer from all three leaders that they would welcome the challenges I'd bring up to improve the business results. I asked each of them if they agreed that my team and I would "own" the final demand signal. They agreed to it, but I am certain they did not fully comprehend what I was asking. Before long, they discovered what I meant.

I accepted the role, which ended up being among the most rewarding experiences of my career. Not only did we significantly improve business results, but it had a positive effect on the culture, and we saw the number of "fire drills" go down substantially. It took a lot of extra time at cocktail hours (I am not complaining), but we succeeded in breaking down organizational barriers that existed, and we improved the business outcome.

For the first time in my career, I could take weekends off from working—and I wasn't the only one!

Although I'm extremely biased myself in this area, I passionately believe that investing in a strong S&OP leader can improve business results. I have found that when a company implements an S&OP process, it either cycles through many managers and gains little traction or becomes a "check-the-box" exercise while the company sleepwalks through the process. Eventually, the process is viewed as non-value added and the cycle of re-energizing or investing in a new S&OP process begins all over again. I believe most S&OP leaders know the "science" behind the process but lack the "art form" to execute it well.

> *I believe most S&OP leaders know the "science" behind the process but lack the "art form" to execute it well.*

If your organization is struggling and is continually focusing on short-term "fires," this is an area to invest in and improve the outcome. If you can have one key takeaway in reading this book, *investing in the proper S&OP leader with broad organizational influence could yield a tremendous business benefit, both tangible and intangible.*

I view the S&OP leader as analogous to a symphony conductor. The conductor must manage musicians and instrumental sections that play different parts yet play the same piece—in tempo, dynamics, and overall harmony (plus they need to able to read music). The conductor needs to understand each instrument and the value it provides to the overall ensemble. The conductor must also understand the strengths and weaknesses of each player and section.

Most important, the orchestra must *trust* the conductor who not only has experience in achieving great music but also listens to the musicians. That is how a conductor emphasizes the intricacies that will make the sound better overall.

> *I view the S&OP leader as analogous to a symphony conductor.*

Like an orchestra conductor, the S&OP lead should possess these same characteristics. When a company can execute well, getting individuals and teams on the same page is extremely rewarding. From there, the mindsets of the S&OP lead and the executive team need to be aligned.

Five key differentiators can "make" a great S&OP leader and should be considered when determining who will lead your process. They are: (1) a collaborative mindset, (2) believing the "means" to the end are just as important as the "end", (3) courage, (4) communicate by simplifying, and (5) possessing a little humility.

First, a key characteristic the S&OP leader needs to possess is a collaborative mindset. This seems to be a no-brainer, but I have seen S&OP leaders focus solely on supporting the process rather than enabling it. This person can be a polarizing figure, eventually failing to improve the business. Just by having an organizational structure unto itself, human beings naturally associate them with that function. They usually have a good understanding of their own function but not a strong understanding of another's function.

How many times have you heard, "I do not understand what (insert name here) does?" This is natural. Everyone must deal with his/her organization's task at hand but may not grasp the value of other teams or individual members. This builds natural organizational walls. A good S&OP leader understands this and invests time developing key relationships, understanding other organizations' value, and learning how other groups are measured and compensated. A good friend of mine taught me a lesson when he exclaimed, "If you want to know how an individual will behave and act, look at what fills up his/her wallet." Heeding this advice, this helped me develop another point of view in which the behavior's exhibited that build organizational walls was a microcosm of an individual's measure of value and ultimately better compensation. It helped put me in the shoes of another person looking at the same issue but from someone else's point of view.

In my view, the means is just as important as the end. Many leaders may have a sense of what to do to achieve the desired result, but they struggle with the path to achieving the result. I have met highly intelligent managers who sensed the best decisions to make but struggled with the process to gain buy-in. These managers were described as combative, non-collaborative ("my way or the highway"), and egotistical. However, when you take away the emotion, the path they want to go down is well thought out for the business's benefit. When it came to yearly performance reviews, behaviors exhibited with negative peer reviews outweighed the decisions that she/he made that improved the business results. This limited career advancement even though the decisions were sound. The manager was polarizing to the organization—either loved or hated, no in-between.

Therefore, hiring someone who has the abilities and desire to put equal focus on the means as well as the end is crucial. Driving a collaborative mindset, having cross-functional team members understand the intent in achieving the result, and listening to other team members leads to creating a collaborative environment. *These are essential qualities for the S&OP leader.*

Eventually, as the leader gains the trust and respect of key team members, many future obstacles will fall. Having someone with high likability in this role is beneficial but not a must. Success comes with being approachable and collaborative, while demonstrating good listening and communications skills.

Another quality a stellar S&OP leader possesses is courage. But not "blind courage," which means challenging every issue that opposes his/her belief. Rather, it is being able to challenge key organizational beliefs and crucial decisions that could negatively affect a customer or a financial outcome. It is important to discern what to challenge and how to do it. For example, an organization had a fundamental belief that Sales are accountable for an accurate demand forecast. (Perhaps this is a key belief in your organization.) Rolling up a Sales forecast contributes to the demand planning process. However, focusing a lot of effort, cost, and time to drive significant improvement in the Sales forecast has never yielded tangible or sustainable improvements (as discussed in previous chapters). Typically, the Sales forecast is leveraged by the Supply Chain to drive blame for a poor business results, citing shortage, inventory excess, or extra supply costs.

At one company I joined, many Sales leaders agreed with me that Sales should not be the only input into the demand forecast; however, the SVP of Supply Chain (the organization I was in) held the belief that Sales owned the demand forecast and needed to be held accountable for a more accurate forecast. By diving deep into the demand creation process, I found many gaps, but the key one was this: No one in the Supply Chain team was even involved in the demand planning process nor attempted to provide input. They were comfortable that they could always blame a poor Sales forecast for all their woes. The organizational blinders were on. Demand planning was owned by Sales and "they" needed to do a better job. Sound familiar? This company invested in measuring every salesperson's forecast accuracy. This approach did not do much to improve the demand forecast.

Given proper focus and attention, this is the one area I know where we could quickly improve business outcomes in cost and working capital. It was another example in which I was accountable for the inventory, on time delivery, and costs, yet had no input into the demand forecast that drove the execution of the Supply Chain. I understood that I would put the SVP's reputation at risk, but I was able to leverage my perceived expertise in S&OP and modify the demand planning process — the Supply Chain Planning team, at the very least, needed to be involved in the final demand forecast.

Incorporating several inputs, I developed a formal change proposal to the demand planning process and met with the SVP of Supply Chain to go through it first - before going public with it. Surprisingly, he stated "this was how it's supposed to work," but clearly it was not happening. I took the blame for the issue so his reputation would still be intact. I would now walk through this change process with other key stakeholder and once aligned, go public — reinforcing how the process should be working.

Amazingly, when I went public to the changes to the Demand Planning processes, I was asked to present my recommendations not only to our C-suite, but to the Board of Directors. I viewed this as a relatively basic S&OP process, but they viewed it as genius. (Again, those who have met me know this is far from true.) There was little experience at the company on what S&OP was and how it should work. The result? Implementing the modified demand planning process quickly improved working capital and inventory turns as well as overall costs.

Yes, calling out and making this change took courage. The turmoil and attention placed on the belief that the Sales forecast was the "root of all evil" put me and in an uncomfortable situation. However, if we did not fundamentally alter the way we managed the process, we would never get out of the vicious circle of blame. If the result did not work out as prescribed, my critics would have pummeled me and put my job and reputation at risk. I was compensated by improving business results, and this had to outweigh any personal fears. I had to "put the money where my mouth was" and not let fear rule my leadership (as I had let happen in my past).

Growing in courage is a journey that does not happen overnight. It becomes a series of successes and failures but a definite characteristic you want in your S&OP leader.

Business is not simple, but to me, there are two types of extreme characteristics individuals can possess when it comes to dealing with complexity. They are either "simplifiers" or, "complexifiers" (not an actual word — yet!). The S&OP leader needs to be a simplifier.

In my experience, a "complexifier" thinks and talks through a lot of variables, throws in multiple obstacles and hurdles, but never reaches a clear, concise conclusion or a recommended course of action. "Complexifiers" struggle to separate relevant versus cursory information. They hope someone else can sort through the information presented to reach a conclusion. Many times, these individuals are perfectionists, making sure every "i" is dotted and "t" crossed.

"Complexifiers" tend to work long, hard hours while getting lost in the myriad of information that needs to be dealt with. Typically, these individuals have a hard time "reading their audience" and believe the value they bring is the detail. They assume they are performing their job on what is being asked of them. Leading meetings, these individuals want to go through each slide without reaching a real conclusion, which eats up valuable time. This person's demeanor, if not well-coached, can lead to apathy in the S&OP process.

"Simplifiers," on the other hand, lean toward finding ways to manage through and communicate complex issues into the essence of the issue, then develop clear, concise recommendations. When preparing for meetings, for example, they will sort through the information and only present relevant points. They focus more on the *quality* of a decision rather *quantity* of information. Their slide decks can be quite big, yet most of the slides are back-up information in case anyone requests more detail.

"Simplifiers" make clear recommendations with alternatives. They bring to the forefront key risk factors and mitigation plans as well as a business recommendation. They can put themselves in the shoes of the meeting attendees and focus on key items they believe should be covered. One of my favorite sayings is, a simplifier "can separate the pepper from the fly shit."

By its very nature, the S&OP function is data rich and can easily turn into information overload. Prepared slide decks for meetings can be well over 100 pages with a lot of content in each slide. A lot of hard work, effort, and scrambling are put into the slide decks; however, it is not practical to cover the entire content of the deck in a two- to three-hour meeting.

The S&OP process leader typically has a monthly audience with members of an organization's C-suite. "Simplifiers" seem to operate more effectively at this level than "complexifiers."

One C-suite executive told me she dreaded the executive S&OP meeting each month, but under my leadership, it became her favorite meeting. The information that was presented was educational and relevant to her. She was able to engage and provide clear direction on the decisions. She also felt she had a good sense of how to manage the risk if the outcome was different from expectations.

Lastly, a terrific trait of a good S&OP leader is having a sense of humility. (It's a good characteristic for any leader.) This person willingly takes responsibility for what goes wrong and gives credit to others for what goes right. He/she develops teams and helps team members analyze and discern information to see what is relevant. He/she is curious and won't jump to conclusions quickly without trying to understand key factors and influencing variables, so he/she can help make the best decisions for the business.

This person builds "bridges" and not "walls" inside your organization. Team members feel comfortable speaking candidly to him/her as they develop trust and partnerships. Not wanting to be put on a pedestal, this person is motivated by improving the overall business outcomes. The "means" to the "end" are just as important as the "end" itself. This person will not perpetuate the "blame" culture and puts his/her ego aside.

These key characteristics of collaboration, focusing on the "means" to the "end" courage, simplification, and humility are extremely important personality traits of your S&OP leader. Yes, ethics, good communication skills, business acumen, and diverse experience should be core competencies, but overlook these personality traits at your peril. People like this do exist, and they might be right under your nose—in HR, Finance, Supply Chain, Sales, Engineering, Operations, Service, Marketing, or other areas.

When you find this leader, traditional rules of grade bands, titles, and compensation packages should be thrown away. Developing positive relationships and trust while building organizational bridges is powerful; the position demands it.

Developing positive relationships and trust while building organizational bridges is powerful; the position demands it.

If this position is not viewed as strategic to your organization, then give it a second look. Where else in the company do you try to balance customer satisfaction, working capital, costs, and revenue in one place where key decisions are made? In a midsize to large company, believing S&OP is the responsibility of the CEO or COO is unwise and not practical.

Your company can hire and develop great individual talent, but a great symphonic performance requires each player to blend and perform collectively. You want to make exceptional music.

Do you have a symphony conductor in your organization?

Chapter 10:
Aligning Like an Orchestra

One of my team members burst into my office to warn me that our country manager was irate. He had just got off a conference call where the country manager screamed at him about how awful the Supply Chain was. He was lambasting the Supply Chain for sourcing product at a higher landed cost than what he committed to in the financial forecast. That meant he'd have to go back and reforecast his numbers. It also meant he'd be off significantly on the profit margin calculation.

Being new at the company, I quickly put together a call with him and key participants in the process. I wanted to understand why we were disconnected, determine the root cause, and decide how we could come together in the future. Before we could get to the issue, though, we had to let the country manager vent his frustrations. He simply could not understand why the Supply Chain team would source higher landed cost product for his territory.

Going through the issues brought these facts to light:

☑ The lowest landed cost supplier (our own factory) had unplanned downtime due to longer-than-usual maintenance and repair activities; therefore, it could not manufacture the supply in time.

☑ The country forecast made assumptions that all of the supply would be at the lowest landed costs and the demand forecast was accurate. However, the forecast was too high.

☑ Third-party supplier agreements were made that if the annual volume was not met, our company ended up with financial penalties.

☑ Other countries in the region had overly optimistic demand forecasts and were allowed to source product at their lowest landed cost for the country, ignoring the regional sourcing plan put together in the S&OP plan.

☑ No one person was orchestrating the planning and execution activities.

☑ Organizational roles and responsibilities had not been clearly defined.

☑ Clearly, all areas of our organization were not aligned.

The sourcing plan for this product was extremely complex. Any financial decision made for the region needed to align with each country. As a whole, the product was almost half of our revenue and was consistently planned for much higher volumes for the region than what actually sold. Unfortunately, sourcing decisions were made based on this erroneous, biased forecast. When it came to execution, each country operated independently to source the product at the lowest landed cost for the country itself and ignored what was best for the region. This ultimately drove higher costs for the entire region. In this case, the irate country manager was negatively affected.

Upon further analysis, I encountered many of the same organizational issues that prevailed in my previous engagements. These seven issues stood out:

1. The "blame game" was in full swing. Sales blamed Supply Chain for bad sourcing decisions, and Supply Chain blamed Sales and Marketing for bad forecasts.

2. The formal S&OP process lacked real teeth, leadership, and false assumptions on what was really happening. The financial forecasts were not tied to the S&OP output even though most people assumed they were. Supply Chain advocated responsibility in demand forecasting to Marketing and Sales, and Supply Chain provided no input to the demand process. Apathy in the process was very apparent.

3. Supply Chain, now under my responsibility, had cycled through several leaders through the past three years, each ending up being dismissed.

4. Organizational roles and responsibilities lacked clear definition for key responsibilities. Constant firefighting with little or no proactivity dominated.

5. Strategic sourcing decisions were performed by Marketing while Supply Chain was viewed as the team that executed agreements. Again, the Supply Chain provided no input into this process.

6. The morale of Supply Chain team members was dreadful. They were afraid to speak up and provide input for the previous regimes ruled by fear. Plus, they were okay with the fact they could always blame another area's decision for a poor result. Internal to Supply Chain, the communication was poor and lacked a good understanding of organizational value.

7. The goals set for the Supply Chain were not relevant to achieving better customer service or cost reductions.

Referencing the symphony conductor concept, we quickly engaged on this issue as a rallying cry to harmonize the demand planning and overall S&OP process. First, our Planning Team not only became engaged in the demand planning process but ultimately became accountable for the final demand forecast. Eventually, Demand Planning was moved into Supply Chain.

Second, driving organizational clarity, we made the Product Planner the orchestration lead who owned the financial analysis to make the sourcing decisions. Coupled with an improved demand forecast with financial trade-offs, this change made the decision-making clearer. Given the uniqueness and complexity of the product sourcing and landed costs, the independent financial forecasts being made by each country, and the lack of alignment, here is what we did. We augmented the S&OP process, adding a sourcing recommendation meeting that included all the Country and Finance Managers who would agree to the best total cost outcome for the region. This change would ensure the country financial roll-ups were aligned to decisions being made. Overall, we saw a visible financial improvement in the region.

Third, clarifying roles and responsibilities not only brought significant efficiencies to the process, but the overall organization was also able to learn and adapt to managing such a complex process with all the supplier agreements. Morale significantly improved. Why? The issues were easier to define and make decisions against. It added positive value to have only one person own and lead the alignment of the sourcing plan. As a result, the organization could put more focus on the issues and not the people/organizations. The "blame game" was quieted.

Day to day, most organizations struggle with alignment. Adopting an S&OP process is expected to help curb this, but even with following the process exactly as prescribed, it can still fail to deliver on the expectations set. Realistically, if more than one person is involved in the process, gaining alignment will be challenging. Why? Organizational clarity, or lack thereof, is a key contributor to misalignment. Often, when an issue comes up and you are asked who has responsibility for it, you hear general responses such as Sales, Supply Chain, Operations, etc. That gives a directional response, but can you pinpoint the issue to an individual or team that owned that responsibility? If yes, then dig a little deeper. Does that person or team agree this issue is their responsibility? Often, you will receive a different answer.

This scenario is not uncommon. Ask "who in my organization has the responsibility for approving the final demand signal?" If you answer, "the CEO, SVP of Sales, or the consensus demand meeting," then dig deeper yet. It would be extremely rare for a CEO or SVP to be involved in the details of the demand signal. Even if you have someone at this level sign off on the demand signal, typically that person is trusting the organization and the process behind it.

Also, the response that this is done "via consensus" does not answer the question. Any lack of definition on ownership and/or false expectations on who should best manage the final demand signal contributes to the vicious circle of blame.

I suggest empowering the S&OP or Planning leader (could be one in the same) to be responsible in determining the final demand signal. Yes, this person needs to be "in" on the detail as well as understand the potential supply and customer impacts of the decisions made. But mostly this person must be comfortable with always being wrong to some degree. This may eliminate most of the candidates, but the message is not to *expect the perfect demand signal* (it is not possible) but to *eliminate and/or align the company on significant demand decisions.* These are the drivers that can severely affect cost, revenue, or both. Thus, this person would drive a demand signal that is "less in the wrong" than what may be currently happening.

Having one individual responsible for one of the most important decisions a company makes will bring out organizational disconnects and drive better alignment. In the process, understanding the end-to-end supply chain process not only improves for that individual but for the entire organization as well.

Also contributing to misalignment is a lack of understanding and clarity about potential business impacts. For instance, how many times have you heard, "if I knew that was going to happen ... "?

Time and time again, I have been in S&OP meetings when issues are brought up and recommendations are made, but their potential consequences are not mentioned. It is assumed they are understood by the decision-makers. The attitude of the S&OP lead could be that the decision was made with the key decision makers; therefore, "they" should understand the potential consequences and trade-offs. This is a dangerous assumption. A strong S&OP leader should clearly articulate the potential consequences of key decisions and provide guidance on what can be done to mitigate an issue if it does occur. Getting aligned on the potential risks may alter the decision and provide another direction as it stirs a healthy debate among those in senior levels of the organization.

S&OP processes are time sensitive. Typically, schedules provide little or no time to adequately analyze the information collected. To me, this element contributes to the lack of clarity on issues and potential business impacts. Time needs to be built into the process to be able to synthesize and determine what the meeting participants need to focus on instead of reviewing the myriad of standard slides used in the S&OP deck. Doing so not only brings efficiency to the S&OP process; it also helps gain adoption to the S&OP process, which improves decision-making.

One thing that helped me was focusing on key changes from the previous S&OP cycle. Observing large changes provided insight on why things changed and what it might mean for the potential business outcome. Doing this took a lot of "noise" out of the process and synthesized the issues on those needing to be discussed. If your S&OP process feels like it "starts from scratch" every cycle, you might consider this approach.

The culture of an organization does contribute to misalignment.

The culture of an organization does contribute to misalignment. Hidden agendas, egos, and even fear of speaking out may be in play. This cannot be overlooked in your S&OP process!

I have been in positions where a senior level executive ran the organization through fear and intimidation, perhaps not even intentionally. Challenging this person's direction, especially in a group setting, would be committing career suicide. It is possible these individuals "speak out of both sides of their mouths" and don't like to be challenged publicly. This is not uncommon. How many times have you seen two completely different sides of a leader—that is, how he/she acts in a public versus a private setting?

Further, a leader may have a completely different view of the shadow he/she casts when compared with public perception. Although an S&OP process will not solve this issue, a good S&OP leader can recognize and figure out ways to gain trust from the leader. Both should have the intention of making the best decisions for the business.

In contrast, an environment that seeks inputs and provides a safe means of expressing opinions focused on the best business outcomes will not only empower the S&OP process; it will ultimately help the broader organization learn and reduce the amount of alignment issues. I have been in situations where "taboo" subjects were brought up, but once they came to light, they could be solved. For instance, a particular salesperson brought up the fact he needed an exceptionally large order to be shipped before the end of the fiscal period to reach a stretch commission target. To qualify for the timing of the commission schedule, we would incur tens of thousands of dollars in expedited costs. The commission payout was much less than the expedited costs. Most important, the customer did not need the product in the expedited timeframe but was doing the salesperson a favor. By recognizing this, a business decision was made *not* to expedite the order and the compensation structure was modified for this case.

Typically, bringing up individual compensation topics are off limits in a public forum, but the environment had reached the point of being a safe place to broach this topic. This decision ended up being the best financial decision for the business and even better for the customer. Further, those individuals involved understood and aligned with the topic.

How can the culture and environment make an impact in your business? Can conversations such as in the previous example happen in your organization? Can it align on what is best for the business? Or is your company culture an inhibiter to this?

I like to look in the mirror first and ask myself these questions:
- Is this the best decision for the business and is it driving conflict?
- If so, what is causing this conflict?
- How do I influence what is right for the business?

▸ Is the financial impact significant enough to bother addressing the issue?

Answering these questions is like having a compass and a map. You understand how you plot where you want to go, and you have a directional tool to keep you on course. This helps drive alignment through any obstacles and new information that come into play while keeping the focus on the destination.

From a culture perspective, the S&OP leader can have an incredible influence on the company culture—one that should not be underestimated. An S&OP leader needs to interface with many departments and organizational dimensions, thus, covering a lot of territory within your company. How this person behaves and manages issues can have a positive or negative effect on your culture. He/she can earn the trust and respect of the organization in these ways:

☑ actively breaking down cultural and organizational barriers
☑ managing conflict through focusing on *issues* versus *people*
☑ possessing the mindset of what is in the company's best interest including customers, both short and long term
☑ feeling accountable to drive the best business outcome with a terrific attitude that will go a long way.

Finally, ask yourself if your S&OP lead is a champion or an inhibitor to organizational alignment? If you said the latter, acknowledge the great opportunity it presents for the individual and the organization to drive improvement.

Chapter 11:
Behaviors and Culture

It was another late night. Earlier that day I told my wife I should be home around 7 p.m. I looked at my computer screen: the time was 11:15 p.m. Unfortunately, this was a common occurrence. As usual, the plan for the day was mired with unexpected fire drills and issues. The Executive S&OP meeting was the next day, and I could not start putting together the slide deck until 7 p.m. As usual, the individuals who submitted key slides "checked the box" and submitted the required format, but the slides were unusable. They had math errors, poor analysis, no clarity on issues, and no recommendations on actions we needed to take. The contributors to the slide deck had all graduated from prestigious universities, yet their slides made little or no sense to me (or perhaps I was too dumb to understand them). Contacting them for clarification in the evening was futile.

Furthermore, our business was in a tailspin. The demand signal that had been submitted for the process three weeks earlier was no longer relevant, because a few large customers decided to discontinue purchasing certain key products.

Feeling victimized, I sensed the devil on one shoulder and an angel on the other. The devil suggested I paste in the slides that were submitted and not modify them. I would invite the contributors to the meeting to explain them in person. If I did this, I would be holding the contributors accountable for what was expected of them and could embarrass them in front of the top brass. Also, I thought, then they would never submit garbage slides like they did again, and I could go home at a decent hour.

Alas, I would not take the devil's advice. I would just be perpetuating the "blame" culture that I was fundamentally opposed to. Besides, it was my responsibility to sort through the myriad of issues and synthesize them into meaningful actions. By listening to the devil, I would be demonstrating to the executive team that I added little or no value.

The angel on the other shoulder told me to recreate the data and fix the slides, even though this would take me into the wee hours of the morning. If I did not have a good grasp on the issue, I could turn it into a discussion point so the relevant functions could weigh in. Prior to the meeting, I would try to connect with the contributors to align on the messaging. I knew we had to make several critical decisions and put action plans around them. These decisions would fundamentally slow down the sourcing and production plans and affect cost assumptions, supplier contracts, and working capital. I also knew the financial forecast we sent to Corporate last cycle now had no chance of being achieved.

I listened to the angel, went ahead, and finally finished the deck around 2:30 a.m., then I sent it out. With the meeting beginning at 10:00 a.m., attendees would have little time to preview the deck, but at least they had it!

After a few hours of sleep, I got in my car and went to work. I was able to contact a couple of the contributors on my way in, aligning with them on the messaging for key issues. Then, as I arrived, I received a message from our Division President's Administrator to cancel the Executive S&OP meeting. No reason was given. In one way, this was a huge relief, but in another way, my insecurities came to the forefront. Did I do something wrong?

I called my manager but couldn't reach him, so I sent him an email saying I was going home to sleep and would connect with him in the afternoon. At home, I crashed. When I woke up, I was able to log into email. (At this time, we only had dial-up technology, which was sporadic at best.)

My fears were realized. I received an email from the Division President, who had copied my manager. The email stated that the forecast submitted to corporate would not be challenged, and I was basically calling the executive team fraudulent. He ended the email with these words: "STOP WASTING MY TIME."

After agonizing over this response, it confirmed to me what I already knew. *This environment was not a culture of trust and integrity.* Even with following the S&OP process exactly as prescribed, the atmosphere at the time would not allow us to face the facts head-on. Like many companies, its culture—behaviors, attitudes, and hidden agendas—thwarted our S&OP process. That is when I analyzed my own behaviors and attitude and was left feeling defeated. From my perspective, I was performing my role for the best interest of the company. If I was blocked from doing this, it was time to move on, which I eventually did.

The best S&OP processes can be implemented, but the company culture *enables* the process. This factor cannot be underestimated. Culture is like oxygen, and life cannot be supported without it. A good amount of oxygen will enable the process to grow, improve, and thrive. A lack of oxygen will eventually kill the S&OP process.

Culture is an overly broad term and not easy to characterize, but it is the behaviors and actions of yourself and others that will indicate if your culture is healthy or unhealthy. To me, there are a few key areas to evaluate which come down to trust, integrity, and curiosity. All three need to work in concert to enable, strengthen, and improve the process.

Trust dies, but mistrust blossoms.
— Sophocles

These words about trust and mistrust from the ancient Greek dramatist Sophocles have rung true throughout humankind. This is reality in business and life today. Earning trust is exceedingly difficult and needs to be demonstrated in both words and actions. Most of us struggle with this when we either breached someone's trust and/or felt violated after trusting in someone. Every time this happens, mistrust can blossom. Before you know it, the organization is made of people who do not trust each other. This contributes to a "blame" culture and gives the S&OP process little chance for success.

It sounds cliché, but the higher in leadership you ascend, the more important it is to earn and keep the trust in the organization. It also becomes harder when there may be several leaders competing for the next promotion.

I have spoken to many people about trust in the work environment. Common statements such as these emerge:

▶ {insert name} is an idiot.
▶ {insert function} does not care about the right decision; they only care if their metrics look good.
▶ This company does not care about me, so why should I care about it?
▶ I have been through X bosses in X years. How can I trust we know what we are doing?
▶ All this person cares about is how he or she looks to higher management.
▶ No one wants my opinion.

These statements point the finger at others, and self-reflective criticism rarely comes up. Furthermore, when I speak to the people being referenced in the quotes above, they typically have similar types of answers.

Unfortunately, there is no fix for this issue; it is basic human nature. However, being conscious of this can go a long way, especially for those in leadership positions. How a leader reacts, behaves, and coaches team members goes a long way toward fostering trust in an organization. Creating awareness and recognition of your own actions that negatively affect culture, which in turn impedes the S&OP process, is a step in the right direction.

Creating awareness and recognition of your own actions that negatively affect culture is a step in the right direction.

For me, gaining trust is important. In a way, it is a selfish motive. I believe if I can gain trust with key members of our organization, people would feel comfortable enough to confide in me about issues they would never bring up in a public or even private setting. Then I could use this information to potentially alter a decision or direction. For example, when the annual sales quotas were set, the amount of business in the sales funnel was always at its lowest point, but after they were set, new opportunities would emerge. This wreaked havoc on the Supply Chain and added significant costs to expediting material for non-visible business. So, with our largest accounts, I was able to establish relationships with key salespeople who gave me insight into what was coming that was not in the funnel. Without calling out the account manager, I could come up with some analysis to begin driving volume that was not yet visible in the funnel. Of course, we would not make decisions that could be potentially harmful, but this insight helped make better decisions overall and took cost out of the business.

This all came down to gaining trust with key team members and not perpetuating blame. This was one way I could understand the reality of the situation and figure out another way to manage it.

> *"In looking for people to hire, look for three qualities: integrity, intelligence, and energy. And if they do not have the first, the other two will kill you."*
> *— Warren Buffet*

Throughout my career, I have had to resist the temptation of personal financial (short-term) gain over broader organizational benefits of a company. I am not perfect in this area, but I am constantly reminded of a few individuals with a lot of energy who were extremely intelligent, but in my view, they lacked integrity.

I have been conscious of not being perceived as one of those individuals; however, I am not that intelligent so I would not make the cut anyway. I reference these individuals as "anti" role models. I keep an eye on their careers as they move from company to company, with the previous company always worse off than they were prior to their arrival.

Without integrity, the decisions made in the S&OP process could drive decisions that cause great financial damage to your company. For me, integrity starts with looking at yourself first while focusing on driving decisions for the greater good. Fortunately, I have stepped away from organizations I felt lacked integrity, no matter how I behaved.

By comparison, decision makers in some companies I have worked in demonstrated high integrity. By far, these were the best places to work in. Politics seemed to be kept to a minimum, and leaders and employees who "stepped out of bounds" were no longer employed by the company. This was a clear message the company would not tolerate unethical or illegal behavior.

In my view, if you do not expect integrity for yourself, you should not expect to find it in others. A healthy culture holds integrity to high standards. Integrity is a key enabler to your S&OP process.

"Be curious, not judgmental."
— Walt Whitman

Curiosity can be a key element in any successful culture. How often are we apt to call an idea idiotic, a person inept, or a recommendation ridiculous? We are all defined by our experiences, but we have not experienced *everything*. In a busy world, we train our minds to see a viewpoint that fits our experiences. Many times, we become judgmental, which crushes any hope of understanding another person's point of view. We then lose the chance to learn something new.

I, for one, have fallen into this trap, but when I become curious, I have a great chance to gain insight and knowledge I did not have before. This insight may change the way I behave, act, and make decisions. Other times, it may reinforce the belief

I already had. Creating opportunities to have individuals feel comfortable in expressing ideas, thoughts, and recommendations can be enlightening. In all, it provides opportunities to learn and potentially change a decision that would have been made differently—all with a goal of achieving a better outcome.

Adopting a culture of curiosity starts with how individual leaders behave, react, and ask questions. I was fortunate to have been with a company that formally invested in developing such a culture. Learning to become curious instead of judgmental has been a game-changer for me. Having been in roles where I always felt on the defensive can put my mood in a bad place. Poor moods can affect judgment and behaviors. Becoming conscious of this has helped me gain knowledge I would not have had before curiosity re-shaped my opinions and decisions. Having this mindset aided my ability to trust, collaborate, and ultimately, be part of better outcomes. Being curious keeps me humble because it points out how much I do not know or understand while also growing my knowledge base.

You might seek out consulting firms that can help your organization implement an S&OP process. The process is prescriptive and, on the face of it, logical. However, if the organization's culture is filled with animosity, dictatorships, and distrust, the S&OP process will fail to meet expectations. This cannot and should not be underestimated. Many times, the culture and the circle of blame that continually exists prompts organizations to invest in an S&OP process. Sometimes, it is formed with the intent to push blame and accountability elsewhere.

If the intent behind implementing an S&OP process is to prove a person or organization "right" versus "doing the right thing," then the implementation is pre-destined to fail. Company culture can be improved, but it does take an investment and a commitment from senior leadership to change and model good behaviors first. I have experienced this, first-hand, and will always be better for it. Have you?

Does your organization's culture allow the S&OP process to be successful?

Chapter 12:
Putting It All Together

For many reasons, company leaders are overly critical of their S&OP processes. Causes of the criticism can include lack of understanding the value the process can bring, continually being challenged with external and internal supply complaints, and never achieving all the financial targets that are set.

However, I have been through many S&OP assessments by third parties and have been skeptical of their conclusions. They include pointing toward poor results and metrics, critical interviews with key stakeholders, and lack of depth of the knowledge of the process that has been implemented—all with the goal to obtain more business for themselves via consulting on process improvements or implementing new tools. Thus, they easily point out flaws and provide critical feedback from many of the constituents who may not grasp the value of the entire process.

It is easy to point to metrics that are not improving and falling short of goals. This is especially true with forecast accuracy. The success or failures of your S&OP process comes down to three basic elements: competency, organization, and culture. To experience sustainable improvement in your company's financials, all three must be evaluated and actively managed.

In my experience, companies struggle with finding the correct leaders for the S&OP process. Given the discipline needed to run it, typically the skills sought in the leader are related to program management. That includes:

☑ developing and adhering to schedules.

☑ ensuring all the data and information presented is accurate.

☑ creating a standard format and template to fill out information.

☑ making sure key metrics are evaluated and measured.

These competencies are important to the process, but many S&OP leaders lack crucial business intimacy. That requires understanding what is valuable to customers, having knowledge of the products and services being sold (including quality issues), and grasping key supply chain competencies. This person also needs to possess excellent interpersonal skills as discussed earlier. Not having these key competencies is like having a nervous system that is partially disconnected from the brain.

An organization needs to be able to support a good S&OP leader with those competencies. Yet companies struggle in this area. I believe the best S&OP leader needs to be viewed as a quasi-general manager and not given a specific functional goal. This is difficult for companies and HR organizations to grasp. S&OP is mostly viewed as a process, bringing together the many functions of the organization to make decisions. To me, this is one-dimensional thinking.

Adding an additional dimension to your S&OP leader with general manager-type competencies can make all the difference in improving a company's financials. This means to attract this type of talent and experience; the organization needs to make an investment outside the traditional scope of its standard organizational design. Doing so would be viewed as a "leap of faith," but it can be a game-changer.

Lastly, the culture and environment need to enable the S&OP process. Yes, you can have competent people and good organizational practices. But if the culture suppresses people's perspectives and seeks to blame rather than understand, it has little chance of setting up a successful S&OP process. This is a fundamental challenge in all organizations, but the behaviors and actions at leadership levels will make all the difference.

A good S&OP process will always encounter some type of conflict—something that should be expected. I have been developing my own methods to address the question "is this the best long-term decision for our business?" I have added this question to my repertoire over time when the organization is trying to make and align on key decisions.

Why would I ask this question when it is assumed that is what we are paid to do? Because we really do not know if this is the best decision. However, this can bring to the forefront personal agendas and logical rationale as to *why* we should make this decision. The key is coming to and aligning to a decision. Not everyone will agree with it, but a decision is not a decision if not followed through.

My hope is that this book can assist you in your organization's S&OP process development and improvements while creating awareness of issues by looking at them from through a different lens. Blame, bias, and apathy, which exist to some degree, but must be recognized and managed.

One of the most paramount decisions your company makes is what to forecast and then execute against it. The lack of focus and attention this gets inside your company may be surprising to you. So far, there is no such thing as a 100% accurate forecast. But you can be assured your business results will improve significantly if you recognize and curb these qualities—blame, bias, and apathy—in your S&OP process.

Glossary

Balance Sheet
A financial statement that reports a company's assets, liabilities, and shareholder equity at a certain point in time.

Best-in-Class
Continually achieving the highest score of a measurement compared to other companies in a given market or industry.

Black Belt (Six Sigma)
A specialist who analyzes business and operations processes for ways to improve business performance.

Board of Directors
An elected group of people that represent shareholders of a company. Responsible to set policies for corporate management and oversight.

Cash Flow
The net amount of cash and cash-equivalents being transferred in and out of a business.

Check the Box
A phrase which means to complete a task at the barest minimum standard and subsequently cease working.

Chief Executive Officer (CEO)
The highest-ranking executive in a company

Chief Financial Officer (CFO)
The senior executive responsible for managing the financial actions of a company.

Chief Operating Officer (COO)

The senior executive responsible with overseeing the day to-day administrative operational functions of a business.

Chipset

Used in computing, this is a set of electronic components in an integrated circuit known as a Data Flow Management System that manages the data flow between the processor, memory, and peripherals.

Commission (Sales)

A key aspect of sales compensation. The amount of money a salesperson earns based on the number of sales they have made for a pre-defined period.

Consensus Demand

A key part of the S&OP process with several cross-functional inputs that develops one demand signal to drive supply chain execution

Consensus Forecast

Also referred as Consensus Demand. A key part of the S&OP process with several cross-functional inputs that develops one demand signal to drive supply chain execution.

Cost

The amount that has to be paid or spent to buy or obtain something.

CPFR

Collaborative Planning, Forecasting, and Replenishment. An approach which aims to enhance supply chain integration between two or more companies that benefits all parties.

C-Suite

Widely used vernacular describing a cluster of a company's most important senior executives.

Demand Forecast

Estimations about future customer demand over a defined period.

Demand Planning

Process of forecasting or predicting future sales orders for products and service.

Demand Signal

Anticipated future customer orders that drive supply chain execution including purchasing, manufacturing, and capacity planning.

Execution Window

A period in time that cannot be significantly altered

Expedite

Make an action or a process happen sooner than planned. Expedites can be costly and disruptive to a business.

Fiscal Period

The period covered by financial reports.

Forecast Accuracy

A measure of deviation between the actual demand from the forecasted demand.

Forecast Bias

Occurs when there is a consistent difference between actual outcomes and previously generated forecasts – either consistently too high or low.

Grade Band

A defined compensation range used by companies for a specific job title.

Incoterms

Series of pre-defined commercial terms published by the International Chamber of Commerce (ICC) relating to international commercial law. Determines when ownership and liability is transferred from one entity to another at each node in the supply chain.

Integrated Business Planning (IBP)
The business planning process based upon S&OP that extends further into customers and suppliers to deliver one seamless management process.

Inventory Reserve
A contra asset account on a company's balance sheet made in anticipation of inventory that cannot be sold above cost.

Inventory Turns
The financial ratio showing how many times a company has sold and replaced an inventory over a given time period. A key variable in defining cash flow.

Key Performance Indicator (KPI)
A measurable value that demonstrates how effectively a company is achieving key business objectives.

Landed Cost
The total charge associated with getting a shipment to its destination.

Lead-Time
A pre-defined time that passes from the start of a processes until its conclusion.

Market Share
The percentage of an industry or market's total sales, that is earned by a company over a specific time.

Niche Product
A specialized product targeting a specific section of a larger market.

On-Time Delivery
A measure of shipping or receiving an order in a pre-defined period of time.

Pre-Consensus Forecast
A series of forecast inputs that are analyzed to determine the consensus forecast.

Planning

A function inside an organization that focuses on future demand and supply needs.

Product Life Cycle

The length of between the time the product is developed and no longer sold. Typically, it is broken into four stages: Introduction, growth, maturity, and decline.

Product Replenishment

The amount of product that is needed for a desired inventory level.

Profit

A financial gain. The difference between revenue and costs.

Profit and Loss (P&L)

A financial statement that summarizes the revenue, costs, and expenses incurred during a specific period.

Revenue

The total amount of income generated by the sales of goods or services. Sometimes referred to as gross sales or "top line.

Sales and Operations Planning (S&OP)

Integrated business management process that focuses on key supply chain drivers including sales, marketing, demand management, production, inventory management, and new product introduction. Foundational process that was refined to more comprehensive planning processes such as Sales, Inventory, and Operations Planning (SIOP) and Integrated Business Planning (IBP).

Sales Inventory and Operations Planning (SIOP)

A modified definition of S&OP that brings inventory into the forefront to enhance the meaning of S&OP.

Sales Order Lead Time   *The latency between the initiation of a sales order and receipt of a product or a service.*

Sell-Through   *The amount of product moved from an inventory location to a customer or consumer over a defined period of time.*

Senior Vice President (SVP)   *A senior-level executive who usually reports to the CEO.*

Service Level Agreement (SLA)   *Defines the level of service expected from your vendor, laying out the metrics by which service is measured. Sales order lead times are often used as a key measure.*

Smokey Bear   *An American campaign and advertising icon of the U.S. Forest Service for wildfire prevention*

Statistical Significance   *A determination that a relationship between two or more variables is caused by something other than chance.*

Stock Keeping Unit (SKU)   *A unique number used to internally track a business's inventory. The number differentiates itself based on the physical elements and features it represents.*

Supply Chain   *A network between a company and its suppliers to produce and distribute products and services to the final buyer.*

Total Addressable Market (TAM)   *The total revenue opportunity available for a product or service.*

Vice President (VP)   *A senior-level executive who is usually is responsible for a specific organization's key function.*

Weeks on Hand Inventory   *A measure of inventory that estimates how many weeks of supply would be available for sale or usage if not replenished.*

Working Capital   *Difference between a company's current assets and liabilities.*

CPSIA information can be obtained
at www.ICGtesting.com
Printed in the USA
FSHW011622131021
85350FS